Therefore; Forgive, Lov
book that demonstrates k
lives of ordinary peop .... *These*
affirming messages of forgiveness, hope, and healing
promote a champion spirit in Christ Jesus.
Pastor Bobby Gibson
Associate Pastor & Pastor, Fellowship Ministry
Oak Cliff Bible Fellowship, Dallas, TX

Life in a fallen world makes no promises of being fair.
Regardless of the path we choose, Life's painful tests await
us all. In "Therefore; Forgive, Love, and Rest" these authors
have provided hope! It is through the transparency of their
tragedies and the love of a faithful Father that readers will
come to be reminded that they are not alone and that God is
forever faithful.
Rev. Tony Scott, ThM
Small Groups Coach, Leader
Oak Cliff Bible Fellowship, Dallas, TX

This book is an invaluable, compassionate and spiritual
harvest of insights that will both excite and challenge the
reader. If the art of living is the ability to turn your mess
into a message or your test into a testimony, the authors of
this book have provided an excellent example of how to
accomplish it. An absolute must read.
Marvin Jones
Executive Pastor of Antioch Baptist Church
Waco, TX

The stories of the divinely connected nine authors are absolutely soul stirring. Each story is emotionally captivating, forcing the reader to reflect on God's grace. The book details real life experiences that mirror spiritual journeys, trials, and tribulations often seen among believers. This book serves as a testament of what happens when you stand firm in your faith despite the circumstance. "Therefore; Forgive, Love, and Rest" will definitely be added to my resource list for clients seeking to find their purpose and make sense of life challenges that make them feel stuck. Nine stories, nine authors, and one well-crafted message...always trust God regardless of "the test."

Dr. Lillian Gibson
Licensed Clinical Psychologist, Denton, TX

"Trust in the LORD with all your heart and lean not on your own understanding." Proverbs 3:5. Therefore; Forgive, Love and, Rest provides multiple examples of Proverbs 3:5. Readers will be able to connect to each testimony to see how the power of prayer and faith can see a person through the most challenging of times.

Lisa Montes, Principal, Almaden Elementary School
San Jose, CA

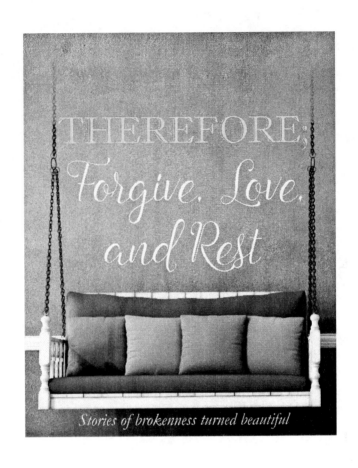

THEREFORE;

Forgive, Love, and Rest

Stories of brokenness turned beautiful

Dena Crecy & More

Dallas, TX

Published by:
Dena Crecy
Dallas, TX
relationshipsgodstyle@yahoo.com

Four Spiritual Laws is an evangelistic Christian tract created in 1952 by Bill Bright, founder of Campus Crusade for Christ, the world's largest Christian Ministry.

TABLE OF CONTENTS

ACKNOWLEDGEMENTS

Thank you God for granting me the courage to pursue this project. I am so grateful to you for having tests that turned into testimonies.

I am so grateful to the co-authors who believed in themselves enough to take this journey with me. Your courage to share your personal story with the world speaks much about your faith in what God has done, and still is doing, in your life.

Thank you to our writing coach, editor, graphic designer, encourager, and much gifted author, Michelle Stimpson for saying, "Yes" when asked to join me in this project. Thanks to Karen McCollum-Rodgers for helping with the project.

To family, friends, church members, and colleagues who have provided prayers, encouragement, and heartfelt support through this journey, thank you for being there to receive H.E.L.P and allow me to share H.E.L.P through the word and love of Jesus Christ. Special thanks to those who took the time to read and endorse this labor of love.

To you who are still hurting in some way, H.E.L.P is here for you. Let us know how we can walk alongside you. We are better together with God.

INTRODUCTION

The H.E.L.P project initiated out of a search for my God-ordained purpose after my divorce. I had accepted Christ eleven years earlier, but even though I was in church and actively serving God, I still felt unfulfilled.

As I continued to pray and cry out to God, He provided sessions on the purposes of God. I learned the general purposes for His creation of mankind: 1) To know God; 2) To be conformed to the image of Christ; and 3) to make Him known. My heart was glad to serve Him in those areas, as I continued to search for my customized purpose.

Houston, Texas is my home. In 1998, I discovered a class at a church that was not my home church called, "Purity with Purpose." It was a 12-week women's discipleship class that emphasized purity with a purpose. It was a fee-based class that concluded with a graduation in the form of a covenant ceremony. It was a deep, spiritual experience. During the 12 weeks, I put all I had into the requirements and God gave me a glimpse of His purpose for me.

My purpose is to provide support to women seeking **help** (**h**ealing, **e**ncouragement, **l**ove, **p**eace and **p**urpose) through a relationship with Jesus Christ. The scripture base is the King James Version of I Peter 4:10, "As every man has received the gift, even so minister the same gift one to another, as good stewards of the manifold grace of God."

As I look back on my life purpose journey, God has allowed me to share H.E.L.P (healing, encouragement, love, peace and purpose) in 4 main areas: Life Purpose, Relationships, Financial Freedom, and Career Development. It has been a grand journey to date. I would not change a thing.

I thought many times that no one else is going through or experiencing what I am experiencing or feeling the way I was feeling. However, every time this happened, God showed me that there is nothing new under the sun. As I became vulnerable and would seek help, OR, when I allowed my pride to cause me to hide from my circumstances, He would ALWAYS send help to remind me that He knows and He does care.

This project is about people being willing to share the God testimonies that came from the God tests. Our prayer is that as we share our hearts with yours you will see the power workings of God and want to experience Him more in your everyday life.

DENA CRECY

"And we know that for those who love God all things work together for good, for those who are called according to His purpose. For those whom He foreknew He also predestined to be conformed to the image of His Son, in order that he might be the firstborn among many brothers." Romans 8:28-29

Working for My Good

This is the story about how my marriage and divorce brought me to an intimate relationship with God, and allowed me to discover my God-ordained purpose.

In the beginning...

I was born on April 6, 1959 in Houston, Texas. There was my mother, grandmother, and three other siblings; a younger sister and two older brothers. We lived in a five-room apartment. My granny died when I was about five or six years old, leaving my mother to raise us alone.

My mother was divorced, and I did not know my father. When I was 13, my mother remarried. It seemed okay, at first. However, he began to come into the bedroom I shared with my sister after my mother went to work, as she worked 11 p.m. to 7 a.m. His behavior was inappropriate with me and I left the house. I went down the street to a friend's house until my mother came home that morning. I explained to her what happened. She asked me to not mention this to my brothers, or anyone, and she confronted him. Of course, he denied it. I was not sure if my mother believed me, because she did not immediately put him out. He left a short time later and she eventually divorced him. Counseling was not an option back then, and the subject was not openly discussed at school. The incident was never spoken of again between me and my mother. We went on with life like it never happened.

In 1976, when I was in the eleventh grade, the husband of a friend that was married during high school, made advances towards me one day while I was braiding his hair. When I questioned what his wife (my friend) would think, he responded, "What about her? I am not trying to leave her; I just like you, too." He also stated that if I didn't go along with his proposition he had other options (women waiting to get with him). It would be better if it was me since I was her friend. The reason we could have that conversation without my friend, is because I would occasionally braid his hair at my house.

Because of my own neglected issues and insecurities I went along with it for a very short time. I began to quickly see that he was going to prey on whoever was willing. I cut it off. I felt horrible, stupid, angry and embarrassed. Why did I allow it to happen? Was I that needy? What was going on with me? Two inappropriate male advances....one rejected and one accepted. From what I had learned growing up so far, fathers (even stepfathers) are supposed to provide and protect. Not to molest. I understood that marriage was between a man and a woman and no extra people should be involved. I knew they both were wrong.

My family moved away and I did not have to see him again. To my knowledge, I don't think my friend was aware of what was going on. We did not stay in touch after I moved and the friendship was lost. I did some soul searching and decided not to date for a while.

Lessons learned:

1. It is never right to date or be with someone else's husband.
2. Set boundaries for yourself and stick to them.

"Do not be deceived: God cannot be mocked. A man reaps what he sows" (Galatians 6:7).

Post High School

After graduating from high school in 1977 I attended University of Houston, downtown campus. In 1978, while visiting a sick friend from my early childhood, Lee, his

4

cousin Andre' was there and asked me out. Andre' was raised with Lee so I was familiar with him. He also attended University of Houston main campus. Andre' took me to see Parliament and the Funkadelics. It was my first concert and I was very excited!

This was the beginning of our relationship. Andre' worked two jobs and went to college. He worked at Church's Chicken during the day and Spec's Liquor in the evening. He took me to the best restaurants Houston had to offer. We spent lots of time together. Sometimes we didn't go out; he would just bring over some chicken and alcohol and we would watch television. He would let me ride with him to run errands, get his hair cut, etc. As time went on our relationship became physical and in the summer of 1979 he offered to get an apartment close to my mother so we could move in together. I quickly let him know that my mother did teach me that if I was good enough to live with, I was good enough to marry. I told him that the next step for me was marriage, as I am a wife.

He said he wanted to get married but was afraid of needles. During this time you had to have a blood test to get married in Texas. I told him to figure it out, as I was not going to just keep on dating him. In the meantime, I was pretty sure he was going to propose, so I talked to my mother about wanting to marry him and asked for advice.

She told me to ask him what his plans or goals were for our marriage. That way, I would know where I fit. She advised me that if I didn't hear a fit I may want to continue dating until a fit is discovered or we learn that we are not a good fit at all. So the next time Andre' and I were together, I started the discussion. It went something like this:

Me: What are your plans or goals for our marriage?

Andre': I'm going to be rich!

Me: What does that mean?

Andre': I don't know. I just know I am going to be rich!

Me: How are you going to be or get rich?

Andre': I don't know. I just know it is going to happen.

Me: What does rich look like? How will you know when you are rich?

Andre': Stop asking me all these questions! I am going to be rich and that's it!

So there you have it! I did not have more information about his plans for this marriage. Did I care? No. He had said that he loved me and that's all that mattered.

We also had discussions about "little things" that we noticed about each other. I asked questions about Andre' not following rules/laws. From traffic laws to just rules in general. His response was that rules/laws were made to be broken. No one was the boss of him. I did not make a big deal out of it because we were still young and hadn't had time to grow and mature.

In the fall of '79, while we were out to dinner, he produced a ring and proposed. We agreed to get married after our 21st birthday the following year. I am one month older than Andre' and he would refer to me as his "old lady."

After my birthday in April, he decided to be brave and go and get the blood test. It took all day with the nurse chasing him around the clinic, but he finally got it done. As we were not in church and did not want a big wedding, we agreed to go to the courthouse and get married on April 18, 1980. I had started with Exxon/Mobile in 1979 and he joined the company at the beginning of 1980. Our coworkers gave us a nice wedding shower. Andre' decided to leave college, saying it was taking too long and he wanted to focus on our marriage and his getting rich goal. I continued to take classes at night. We had our careers set and I thought this was the beginning of a beautiful relationship.

Lessons learned:

1. Pay attention to the advice of your parents.
2. Pay attention to the "little things" that stick out in the relationship.
3. Don't rely on your feeling to guide you because they are often clouded by physical attraction.

The Marriage and Separation

Things went well the first few years. We were both working for Exon/Mobile, at the same campus, but different buildings. We built a new construction home, had a car and a truck, had a huge savings account and lived on a budget. Andre' was very good at managing and saving money, but he wanted me to keep the checkbook. Yes, in the '80s there were no debit cards and we wrote checks. I had not learned budgeting or money management, so like clockwork, Andre' sat me down on the 16th and the last day of the month, after each payday, for me to go over the checkbook and what the accounts looked like. That accountability of having to explain kept me in check. We still had the same "little issues" that we discussed before we got married, but life seemed to be good.

In 1983, I begin to notice a tug from God. I started asking co-workers where they went to church. I explained that I was looking for a Bible-believing, Bible-teaching church. After visiting several churches, in the summer of 1984 I gave my life to Christ, joined Lakewood Church and was baptized by Pastor John Osteen. Andre' was not interested in church, but did not mind me going. As a new Christian, Lakewood Church was too large for me, so I found a smaller church which I joined a month later. Pastor Willie Jones and his wife Mary taught the new member class. It was a 12-week class. Pastor Jones taught 6 weeks and Mary taught 6 weeks. It was very intense. I was learning a lot.

In 1985, Andre's mother, who lived in California, died. Though he had never been close with his mother, he still had a lot of mixed feelings about her death that he did not want to share with me or anybody. Shortly thereafter, he lost his job at Exxon and things began to go downhill. His bent toward not following rules or the law went full force. He took to the streets and began living a life that was contrary to both God's law and the law of the land. Hustling became his full time job.

The hustling situation was more than I could deal with. Back then, pagers were the popular form of communication and his went off all the time. Every time it went off he would leave. He was in and out all times of the day and night. He was fencing stolen goods and selling drugs. I never knew if he was going to come home or what.

He did not bring anyone to the house, at least not that I knew of, but would definitely leave when that pager went off. It did not matter where we were or what we were doing, when the pager beeped, he was gone.

I constantly worried that something might happen to him out there on the dangerous streets. It was hard to sleep when he was not home. After barely completing the spring semester at University of Houston, I decided I couldn't go back anymore. With all the drama at home, it was hard to concentrate. I had earned just over 60 hours.

After being on birth control for over 10 years, in the summer of 1985, my doctor took me off due to some complications. I asked him what were the chances of me getting pregnant and his response was, "It could take a while." In my mind I was thinking, well since Andre' and I are having problems, God would not let me get pregnant. I was more concerned with STDs.

Yeah, right...I was back in his office 6 weeks later— pregnant. In the meantime, I had decided to file for divorce. However, I did not know that in the state of Texas, you could divorce while you were pregnant. That was a $400 lesson. My son, Andre' Sean Crecy, was born on April 20, 1986. I gave him a middle name since his dad does not have one. We called him Sean.

The relationship was touchy, but we tried to stay together. My mother passed away suddenly of a heart attack in October 1987. I felt that my best friend had died. My mother and I were very close. Andre' and I were moving further away from each other.

I talked to Pastor Jones, who advised me that light and dark cannot dwell together. The harder I prayed the further apart Andre' and I became. I suspected that he was having an affair. There were subtle things that were happening. He did not want to spend time with his immediate or extended family. He started going "fishing." I knew he did not know how to and had no interest in fishing. He didn't own a fishing pole or any kind of fishing gear. And then in 1988, when I was ready to see it, God revealed it to me. My husband was having an affair.

When I questioned him about it, his response to me was that it was true. He said that he did not love me anymore and his heart was with this other woman. He actually said that he knew her first, as if that was supposed to make a difference. He then went on to explain that she supported him and his street life in a way that I did not. The conversation went something like this:

Me: (Crying) What about our marriage vows?

Andre': I don't know what your problem is. She knows about you and is okay with it. You are the one that is tripping. All you have to do is think of me as being a merchant seaman, away on a boat for 6 months. I will eventually come home.

Me: I did not sign up for that and cannot do that. I signed up for a marriage with one man and one woman, nothing else. (Sobbing) What about Sean?

Andre': I'll see him. He will be alright. Why don't you fight for me? If you love me you would fight for me. I told you where she lives. You say you are a Christian woman. I thought you were supposed to submit to your husband.

Me: Really? You are going to say that to me? If you are going to quote scripture, at least get it right. The Bible says wives submit to your own husbands as unto the Lord. You are not submitting to the Lord. I am not going to be in the streets with you and our son. Why would I fight for something I already am? I am already Mrs. Crecy. And I am not going to misrepresent the Kingdom of God by acting like that. Don't get me wrong, I want to go a round or two with both of you, but I'm not going to do it. (Still sobbing and yelling) How could you do this to me… to Sean?!!!! If I have to choose between you and God, I choose God."

He left and I was devastated.

I went into a deep depression. I felt like there was a deep hole in my stomach. I could not function. I was crying all day, every day, at work. I would spend most of my workday in the bathroom. A co-worker, Cynthia, started coming in the bathroom to check on me. She would hug me and just pray with me. She was a Godsend. She never asked what was going on, but suggested that I take a 30-day leave and get some help, so I did.

I began counseling with Pastor Jones by myself. Andre' said he was not going to counseling, ever, because it was for white people. I thought the counseling sessions were going to be focused on Andre', since he was the one cheating and hustling, but the focus was on me. Pastor Jones asked me if I was the suitable helper that the Bible spoke of. I quickly tried to direct him back to Andre' and all the non-husband-like things he was doing, but Pastor Jones was not having it. He continued to ask me about my role. He said Andre' is not here, but you are.

During the counseling sessions quite a few things were brought out. He asked if Andre' had moved out, and I said, "Not really." His things were still there, but he did not come home every night. And when he did come home, I was not cooking or washing his dirty clothes. Let *her* do that! All we did was argue when he came home. My feelings and emotions were in charge.

He said if I was going to allow him to stay, if I wanted God to come in, I needed to be a wife. It took a little time for me to allow God to manage my feelings, but I did. I would have food prepared so when he came home I just had to warm it. At first, he would not eat it as he thought I put something in it. But then he ate it, because he said he enjoyed my cooking so he would just take his chances.

I went back to work after the 30 days and tried to keep it together. During the next few years of our separation quite a bit took place. I will list some because all of it is enough material to write a separate book.

I received many phone calls at home and at work from the mistress. She also wrote letters. Her petition was that Andre' did not love me and I should just go ahead and divorce him. My response was that she was trying to be what I already am, Mrs. Crecy, "and right now, it ain't all that." I also pointed out that he had not served me with any divorce papers at that time. I wanted to say other things but the Holy Spirit would not let me. She even asked why I didn't curse her out or something. I told her that I had to represent the Kingdom of God no matter how much it hurt.

During one of our conversations, I shared with her the commandments that mention adultery and to not covet thy neighbor's house, wife, animals or anything that belongs to thy neighbor. I explained to her that I was her neighbor. Her response was she prayed for a man and Andre' was the man that was consistently in her life. I shared with her that God did not answer that prayer, as God cannot go against Himself. She left me alone for a while after that. ***"Be subject therefore unto God; but*** *resist the devil,* ***and he will flee from you"*** (James 4:7).

One of my counseling sessions with Pastor Jones really messed with me. He asked me if I was I going to file for divorce. I was shocked that my Pastor was asking me about divorce. He said, "Andre' is gone and is openly living with this woman. He has abandoned you and your son and committed adultery. Those are both grounds for a biblical divorce."

I said, "I have not received a release from God and will not file for divorce until I do."

He said that maybe my feelings for Andre' were so strong that I could not hear from God.

I could not deny that but said, "I believe I will know when/if it is time."

He then asked me why I wanted God to save my marriage.

Another shocker! The answers I came up with had nothing to do with God and his kingdom, but me and my feelings and my family.

He asked me why God should save my marriage when it had nothing to do with Him. Wow! I had no answer.

He then challenged me to read everything the Bible had to say about marriage, and then go to a Christian bookstore and ask Him to show me books to read on marriage. I did and it was very enlightening. It gave me a different perspective on God and His creation called marriage. I wanted the marriage I read about.

God, through Pastor Jones, began to send women for me to comfort who were going through bad relationships or marriages. It was very upsetting because I did not understand what was going on. I would share God's word with them, as that was all I had, and they were helped. Their relationship would lead to marriage or their marriage would get better. This was very annoying, as my relationship was still to'-up-from-the-flo'-up.

I spent much time in prayer, crying out to God about my marriage every day and every night. I was praying for Him to zap Andre' like He did Paul on the Damascus road. I opened up my heart and soul, confessing sins and pouring out my feelings. I confessed anger, confusion, and total despair. One night, as I was emptying myself out to God, I felt hugged. I was hugged by God. I knew at that moment, He loved me and all things were working for my good.

Andre' and I went back and forth for a few years. In the spring of 1990, he came by one evening after I got home from work. He rang the doorbell and I let him in. There was a different kind of peace over the house that night. I cooked dinner while he read the paper and played with Sean. We ate dinner; he bathed Sean and put him to bed. We made small talk and watched TV like there was no conflict between us at all. We went to bed and made love. I knew immediately I had conceived a child.

I called my sister-in-law at 3 a.m. to talk to her, as I could not sleep. I poured out my feelings to her about being a single parent so I know God would not allow me to get pregnant now. I didn't want to be a single parent with two children. I believed that was not supposed to be my destiny. My granny was a single parent, my mother was a single parent and now I was a single parent. I believed that since I was in church and reading/studying the Bible, my married life had a better chance than my granny's and mother's did. It was not supposed to be my destiny. When Andre' woke up the next morning the war was back on. The peaceful cloud had left. We exchanged unkind words and he left.

I told myself that I was not pregnant and went back to the same lawyer that I went to earlier to file for a divorce again. A short time later, my doctor confirmed that I was pregnant. I was too embarrassed to tell the lawyer that I was pregnant again, for the same husband, but I had to. She said it must be a sign from God and gave me my money back this time. I told her it was a sign that God wanted me to have two children with my husband, that's all. I was at work crying every day, again.

I gave Andre' the news. He then apparently shared it with his mistress because she sent me a huge bouquet of roses and balloons to the job with a card that read, "Congratulations!" She then began calling again to say that I could divorce Andre' and he would still take care of his children. I said, "Yes, like he is currently taking of Sean today." *NOT.* No child support, financial or otherwise.

The first four months of the pregnancy, I just stayed in the bed all day, barely attending to four-year-old Sean. Here we go again… -another leave from work. This time it was much longer than 30 days. Praise God for great companies like Exxon/Mobile that have wonderful benefits. I had been there since 1979 and they helped me through some tough life situations. My mother always told us to get on a job and build tenure, so when life happens, and it will, you will be able to sustain and still get paid. She modeled the way, staying on her job over 30 years before she retired. We all took my mother's advice on that subject.

We had a women's ministry at the church with subgroups. I was part of the Ruth Circle. Different women from the group would call or come by and check on me, but I would not answer the phone or the door. Two of the ministry leaders came by, Nancy and Regina, and knocked and rang the doorbell. I did not move. They then came to the window and yelled that they would call the police if I did not open the door. So of course, I got up and opened the door.

They put me in the shower. When I stepped out and looked in the mirror, I scared myself. I was so thin and sickly looking. They dressed Sean and me and then took us out the house for a bit. Sean was glad to be outside. He was such a good little boy. He stayed by my side playing with his toys and not saying much, hardly ever crying.

They nurtured me through the pregnancy and Sydney was born in January 8, 1991. She came here feisty and has been feisty ever since.

In 1990, during the pregnancy with Sydney, Andre' was arrested. He was incarcerated when Sydney was born. This began Andre's many years spent in and out of jail. Unfortunately, he has spent more time in than out. As of this writing, in August of 2015, he is serving time in federal prison. His current release date is listed as 2024.

During this time we (or should I say, I) lost the home and both cars. I depleted the savings trying to maintain the same life style. After 2 years, I still had to move, but with nothing. The life we built was based on two salaries and now the kids and I we were down to just mine. My church owned some apartments that they rented out and we were able to move into one. It was a blessing!

I stayed off work until a year after Sydney was born. In January of 1992, after much prayer and counseling, I decided to resign from Exxon/Mobile and stay home to work on me and be there for my children. The money from Exxon would give me a year to work through some things.

A year had passed, so quickly I might add, and it was time to go back to work. In June of 1993, I took a part time customer service job with Chase bank. My schedule was 10 a.m. to 2 p.m. I had purchased a small truck and was off to a good start.

Lessons learned:

1. God does love me AND all things are working for my good.

2. God ordained and has a plan for marriage, between a man and a woman, learn His plan.

3. It takes many hands to help marriage function the way God intended for it to function.

4. Read and apply what the Bible has to say about love and marriage.

5. When faced with a choice between the love of man and serving God, choose God, every time.

6. Do not attempt to do it alone.

7. When the ship is sinking, take the life raft and get off. Instead of using up all the savings trying to save some dignity, I should have sold the house and moved into an apartment.

8. Regardless of the circumstances, God alone gives life. Do not reject it.

9. Church membership, along with serving in ministry, can save your life.

Divorce and Life After

1995: After being separated for 7 years, I heard God's voice releasing me from the marriage. I could not afford an attorney, so it was me and God. My Ruth Circle sisters and friends gave me a surprise birthday party and supplied me with the money to file for divorce.

Andre', still in prison, signed the waiver and returned it to me. But soon thereafter I received a letter stating that he had changed his mind. He wanted to renege on the waiver. I wrote back informing him it was too late.

An attorney friend of my brother filed the petition for me in May. I spent many hours in the law library and was ready to appear before the judge in July. The judge asked about an attorney and I informed her there was not one. She reviewed paperwork, made edits and advised me to come back in a week with the suggested revisions. WOW! I made edits and was divorced a week later, July 18, 1995. I would like to point out that after the divorce, and after all the drama, Andre' never married the mistress.

The church apartments we were living in were very old and had developed mold. I became sick from the mold and had to move. The problem was since I was only working part time, I could not afford traditional apartment living. It looked like I would be homeless. I began to feel sad and decided that I did not want my kids to live on the streets with me, so I was going to drop them off with my mother-in-law and live in my truck.

Little did I know that God was having no part of my plan. I have a good friend that I met in high school, who now lives in Arizona, named Delores. As land lines were the thing and long distance costs were real, we only talked every now and then. She called me the night I was making my plan. I was cleaning the apartment and had packed the kids clothes, when the phone rang. She asked me how I was doing, and of course I said, "Fine."

She asked twice and I repeated the same lie.

She said her mother wanted to speak with me and put her on the phone. Her mother, Julia Coleman, pastors a church in Phoenix, Arizona and has a strong discerning spirit from

God. She began to speak to me and say, "Don't you give up; God loves you and those children and has a plan for you. Don't you quit on God." That is the main part that I can remember. I began to sob thinking, *How could she know?* I did not share with anyone what I was planning to do, just God. That phone call showed me that God really did love me and wanted me to continue to seek Him for a place to live.

I listened to Christian talk radio every day. The next day, while listening to the radio, I heard a gentleman by the name of Dr. Collins being featured. He discussed a program he had called, Footprints in the Sand. It was a transitional living property that had two bedroom, single family homes on it. He helped women who were leaving battered relationships or recovering from drugs.

I felt God nudging me to call and talk with him. I told God, "I don't meet the criteria the man stated on the radio." Yet, I called anyway. I met with him after work the following day and shared my story. He asked me how much could I pay, and I said $200. He showed me a home that had just been completely renovated. It looked brand new!

He asked, "Do you like it?"

I said, "YES!"

He asked me when we could move in. WOW! Look at God! We moved in that weekend.

Right after the move, I felt God nudging me to leave my church. After all that had happened there, it was time to totally move on. I talked to Pastor Jones and he understood. I began to look for a new church home. The leaders from my Ruth Circle group had already moved to a new church home, but we stayed in touch. I visited one of them at their church, loved it and joined. I became a proud member of Community of Faith, where James Dixon, II was senior Pastor.

I served as a Disciple of Christ where we received people who came down to accept Christ during each service. Since Footprints in the Sand was a transitional living property, it had a curfew. Meeting the curfew would not allow me to serve. I met with Dr. Collins and shared my concern to see what we could work out. He spoke to Pastor Dixon and I was entrusted with a key to the property. Praise God!

1996: A full time Customer Service Representative opportunity opened up at Chase in the spring and I was promoted to a Training Specialist in November. I learned through volunteering that training and developing people was part of my purpose. Things were looking up.

1998: I began to seek God for my unique purpose. I felt there was more I was created to do for God and His Kingdom. I was asked by Pastor Dixon to lead the prayer line for the television ministry he was starting in January 1999. It was quite an honor.

1999: My pursuit of purpose search led me to Windsor Village United Method Church, where they had a program called, "Purity with Purpose." It was a fee-based, 12-week women's discipleship program. It was a powerful ministry headed by the Director of the Counseling Ministry. This class changed my life! I signed up to volunteer for the spring session and for the certification program offered. I completed my first year of service as a Prayer Line Coordinator for Pastor Dixon's television ministry.

During the class I discovered my life purpose. It is to provide support to women seeking **help** (**h**ealing, **e**ncouragement, **l**ove, **p**eace and **p**urpose) through a relationship with Jesus Christ. The scripture base is the King James Version of I Peter 4:10, "As every man has received the gift, even so minister the same gift one to another, as good stewards of the manifold grace of God."

My manager at Chase asked me to consider a position as Training Manager for a new site they were opening in Arlington, TX. It would be a promotion.

2000: I prayed about the promotion opportunity, discussed with my children and Pastor and accepted the opportunity. Chase was paying for the move, and I scheduled it for July 3rd. In the meantime, I traveled back and forth to assist with the set up. I completed the spring session as a small group facilitator for the Purity with Purpose class, as well as the certification. It was truly a blessing. While getting settled in the DFW area, one of the leaders from the Purity with Purpose group in Houston reached out to me about a couple of ladies who wanted to start a class and needed help. The Lord blessed me to co-facilitate with 2 different groups here.

2001: In the spring, God blessed me to lead my own Life Purpose group. Ladies in the office were asking me what I did outside of work. Before I knew what was happening, 10 women from Chase had signed up for the class. The Life Purpose class is fee based as there are textbooks and materials, so I was very surprised when people just started giving me money. As I was not totally prepared to lead my own group, I watched God work out everything that was needed, from getting the books ordered and delivered on time, to a place to hold the class and the graduation. God confirmed that this was truly my calling. It was amazing!

After relocating, I began to search for a church home. I visited some of the popular mega churches in the area. Pastor Jones encouraged us to listen to Dr. Tony Evans and other pastors who were on the radio. We even came to Dallas when Dr. Evans did family conferences. I told myself then that if I ever moved to the area I would join his church. I tried to find it one evening after work and got lost. It was dark outside and I gave up. After picking up the kids and traveling home one evening, we were listening to Dr. Evans.

Sean, who was then 14, said, "Why haven't we visited that church?

I said, "I tried to find it but got lost."

He said, "Since you listen to him every day you must like him, so why don't you try again?"

WOW! So I decided we would all go Sunday morning, to the 10:50 service. I mapped out the directions and we came right to it. When we walked in I knew this was it… my new church home. I joined and began a new journey with God.

Andre' and the kids…

Sean at 17 and Sydney at 16 each asked and had an opportunity to go and live with Andre' during one of his "free times." They both only stayed a few months and then returned back home.

Sydney asked why I didn't tell her that Andre' was like that. According to Sydney, Andre' was living with one woman, while he paraded her around Houston to help him meet other women. Then asked her not to mention the others, or lie if she was asked about them. I told her she had to see her father for herself.

As Sean is five years older than Sydney, he already had an idea of what to expect from Andre' and thought he could handle it. He and Andre' got into a big fist fight and that was it.

Andre' writes from time to time and asks about the kids. At this time, they choose not to write or go see him.

Dating?????

In case you are curious, I dated a couple of people after my divorce, but nothing serious. I made a decision to just be still and wait on God. I am committed to living a life pure and holy for Him.

Life Purpose Classes

God afforded me the opportunity to become a Certified Life Purpose Coach in 2008, through Life Purpose Coaching Centers International, where Dr. Katie Brazelton is the founder. I set up Relationships God Style as a non-profit in 2010, and filed and received 501c3 status as of June 2015. God moved me from Chase in April 2007 and placed me at Capital One Bank in August of that year. A reorganization took place and I was laid off in August 2015. As part of the severance package, retraining money was provided to take a course. As of this writing, I am taking the Professional CLPC track with Dr. Brazelton, to be completed in November. The money paid for the entire course! PRAISE GOD! I have written curriculum to start class in the spring of 2016. My dream is to have a Life Purpose Coaching Center that offers faith based life purpose, relationship, financial stewardship, and career coaching. Please join me in praying and believing God for this effort. If you are in the DFW area, you can also sign up to take one or all four courses.

Main lesson learned:

"And we know that for those who love God all things work together for good, for those who are called according to His purpose. For those whom He foreknew He also predestined to be conformed to the image of His Son, in order that he might be the firstborn among many brothers."
Romans 8:28-29

About Dena Crecy

As a speaker, author and coach, Dena has a unique way of connecting with her audience. Her teachings can diagnose the root cause of life issues, while sharing practical, life-changing wisdom on living everyday life. Dena uses humor and shares her own story as part of her authentic approach.

Dena's passion and life purpose is to provide support to women seeking **help** (**h**ealing, **e**ncouragement, **l**ove, **p**eace and **p**urpose) through a relationship with Jesus Christ. Her approach is based on I Peter 4:10, "As every man has received the gift, even so minister the same gift one to another as a good steward of the manifold grace of God."

Dena earned a certification in Training and Development from the University of Houston in 1997. She became a Certified Life Purpose Coach in 2008 with Life Purpose Coaching Centers, International. Dena earned a Master of Science in Theological Studies from Grace International Seminary in 2011. She is also a licensed and ordained minister. Dena is the author of "A Suitable Helper: A Good Steward of God's Resources." The book is available on

Amazon and Kindle, as well as the bookstore of Oak Cliff Bible Fellowship Church in Dallas, TX.

As a speaker and author, Dena is available for your next conference, retreat or gathering. Dena is also available for individual coaching and can be reached by email at relationshipsgodstyle@yahoo.com, or by phone at 469-523-1434.

Awaiting her King, Dena resides in Dallas, Texas. She is the mother of two adult children, Andre' Sean Crecy and Sydney Paulette Crecy. She is the grandmother of Sydney's two boys, Jaden and Kayson.

JEANNETTE DIXON

Let me hear of your unfailing love each morning,

For I am trusting you.

Show me where to walk,

For I give myself to you.

Psalm 143:8

Rest in God's Unfailing Love

Trust God

Throughout life we will face disappointments, letdowns, injustices, heartaches, unfair circumstances, and downright *never imagined in a thousand years, you-"could-do-this-to-me"* type situations. Perhaps you are dealing with a disappointment like this right now. The intensity of your pain may lead you to feel isolated or distant from God. However, take solace in His truth that he cares for you. When blustery winds prevent you from clearly seeing God, rest and take comfort in knowing that He **sees** you. Keep your eyes fixed on Jesus and let Him guide you safely through your storm.

We are reminded in Joshua 1:5, "No man shall be able to stand before you all the days of your life. Just as I was with Moses, so I will be with you. I will not leave you nor forsake you."

What do you do when the most debilitating pain that you have ever experienced comes from the person whom you trusted with your love and your life? My first defense was to deny what was happening, but eventually I had to acknowledge reality.

My season of despair and heartbreak came from my husband whom I trusted with my love and my life. Trusting another person, especially a spouse, indicates that you will always seek to do what is best for each other. Trust is the cornerstone that close relationships are built upon.

I longed for God to make the heartache and pain stop. However God was longing for me to cast (throw) *ALL* my burdens upon Him and leave them with Him. Eventually, I came to realize that my efforts to make matters better resulted in me trying to control a situation that I had no control over. According to Matthew 11:28, God commands believers to, "Come unto me, all that labor and are heavy laden, and I will give you rest."

Growing Up

From an early age, I grew to understand and value the power of prayer from listening to my Mother pray daily. I accepted Jesus into my heart when I was young, and through the years have developed a closer relationship with God through prayer, meditating on His word, Bible studies, small group connections, and reading inspirational books. I know the closer I get to God the closer He gets to me. Therefore, my daily walk is a journey with total dependency upon Him.

Education

After being in the military for twelve years, I attended and graduated from the University of Southern Mississippi. Later, I pursued my master's degree from Argosy University while continuing my career in education.

Marriage

In 1992 while attending Cathedral of the Holy Spirit in Georgia, I met my husband. We married later during that same year. We were both Christians and actively participated in ministry at our church.

New Church

A job transfer relocated us to Dallas, Texas in 2001. After visiting several different churches in Dallas, my husband chose Oak Cliff Bible Fellowship (OCBF), as our new church home, where Dr. Tony Evans is the Senior Pastor.

Spiritual Growth

After completing our spiritual growth classes, we became official and active members of OCBF church. Shortly after that we became Couple's Ministry Leaders, connecting with other couples monthly to study, discuss, and grow in the Word of God. We developed friendships and maintained accountability in our marriage.

From 2001 to 2009

We continued to grow spiritually, as we participated in various ministries at our church.

In 2009 something happened that would turn my life upside down. I had heard and read about couples who experienced divorce after being married for many years. I never imagined I would come face to face with such a tragedy. From my perspective my marriage to my husband represented what a Godly marriage should look like. We worshipped together, we prayed together, we fellowshipped with other couples, and we enjoyed family vacations together. We shared our holidays between both families, and life was good.

Of course, we know that no marriage is perfect, but our friends would often tell us they regarded us as a perfect Godly couple. My husband was my good friend. I depended upon him for so many things. I adored being a wife and was proud that my husband was my protector and the head of our home. We each vowed to love and to cherish each other…in sickness and in health...until death do us part.

December 2009

In 2009, we enjoyed celebrating Christmas with our family. Although it was a joyous time, I began noticing that my husband seemed distant and testy. The distant became much more obvious over the next several months. His demeanor was changing; it was different. My husband isolated himself from the family, emerging from his home office occasionally to have dinner with us.

I complained that he seemed isolated. My husband was concerned his company might be laying off employees, and he anticipated that he might get laid off. I thought perhaps he had been preoccupied with these thoughts. God had always been faithful to us, therefore I had no reason to believe this time would be any different.

Marriage, 2010

As the New Year arrived, my husband was laid off, but he became active in seeking new employment. As he searched for a job, things didn't seem as tense.

I didn't ask many questions, but just tried to encourage, support, and reassure him that everything would be just fine. I didn't analyze the "red flags" that could have indicated that something was deeply wrong, other than the stress of job hunting.

Over the next few months, however, our relationship became visibly strained. I walked on eggshells when I was around him, making sure that I was not saying or doing anything to cause him any additional stress. Individuals in our Couple's Ministry had noticed his distant behavior toward me during our monthly meetings.

New Job, February 2010

My husband soon found employment with another company. I was excited and so grateful to God for two reasons. First, God once again showed us grace and His faithfulness by providing my husband with a new job. Second, I was eternally grateful to God because I saw the new job as a hopeful sign that could eliminate the strain on our relationship.

Announcement, April 2010

Shortly after my husband became employed with his new company, he informed me that he had decided to move out of our home. There was no discussion about his decision. Naturally, I was shocked and in disbelief. I begged him to consider how devastating his decision would be to us and our family. I reminded him we made vows to love and be together until death do us part.

After announcing he was planning to move out, I became distraught, sobbing uncontrollably. My husband sat holding me on the couch trying to comfort me. Even that was perplexing to me because the unexplainable pain that I was in was a result of what he had just told me. Nevertheless, I allowed him to sit, hold, and try to comfort me because I grasped for anything that appeared to be a glimpse of hope in preventing him from abandoning his family.

July 2010

During this time my husband was still living at home. Although he announced he was leaving me and our home, he continued going to church with us, sitting next to me as we worshipped. I was prayerfully hoping and believing every interaction, including our church attendance, was a hopeful sign he was finally seeing his decision to leave me and our family would be devastating, not only for our family, but also for the Kingdom of God.

During the Fourth of July holiday, we had a combined family (his family and my family) gathering at my mother's home in Mississippi. My husband said he could not attend during that time because of his work schedule. I accepted his excuse for not attending the family gathering and tried to remain positive. I was prayerfully thinking that maybe he needed some time by himself and that upon my return from Mississippi, things would finally be back to normal. That proved not to be the case.

Return from Mississippi

Upon my return from Mississippi, my husband informed me while we were gone, he found an apartment, and would continue his process of moving out of our home.

I spiraled back into a state of shock and disbelief. I became visibly upset, sobbing uncontrollably as before. He thought I should lie down and rest so I would not make myself physically sick. Sleeping was the last thing I wanted

43

to do. I was baffled. I didn't understand how my husband could tell me he was leaving, and then turn around to try and comfort me after giving me such devastating news. I struggled desperately in all of this confusion to understand why and how he could make this kind of decision. I was simply perplexed. Two things were certain: my state of desperation did not move him to do the right thing for me or our family; and his decision was not a Godly one.

1 Corinthians 14:33 says, "For God is not the author of confusion..."

September 2010

In September my husband asked me (us) to attend an out of town football game. I was excited to do so, anticipating what I thought would be a positive outcome while we laughed, held hands, and talked as if nothing was wrong. After the game we drove back to our home early Sunday morning. Later in the day my husband announced this was the day (Sunday) he was "transitioning" out of our home. He also explained to me "nothing" would change. I didn't see how that was possible. He made a decision to leave me (our family and our home). I wondered how things could be the same when the leader of the home was leaving. I loved my husband and could not wrap my mind around decisions he was making. It simply did not make sense, but he followed through and left our home.

That Sunday as I watched him loading his car with clothes, my body felt lifeless. I felt desperately lonely and alone, and couldn't tell anyone why I was feeling that way because I shuddered at the thought of anyone knowing my husband was leaving his family.

Many times I attempted to remind my husband what scriptures said about abandonment and marriage. He abruptly reminded me he knew what the bible said, and I didn't need to tell him. Instead, he said God wanted him to be happy. God speaks specifically about marriage in His word. **Matthew 19:4-6 says, "Have you not read that he who created them from the beginning made them male and female, and said, "Therefore a man shall leave his father and his mother and hold fast to his wife, and the two shall become one flesh. So they are no longer two but one flesh. What therefore God has joined together, let no man separate."**

Moved Out of the Home

After his departure, he continued to come to the house, using the key to let himself in and out whenever he pleased. At that time, I had not shared with anyone other than family members that he had left. He called and visited frequently. My husband's actions were confusing to me. He told me that he was leaving me, which included our home and our family, but he called frequently and came to our house daily. I loved my husband, and allowed every visit and phone call because I thought, "the big turn-around" would happen at any moment. He called every Sunday morning to make sure that we were up and planning to attend church. He came to church every Sunday and sat next to us as we worshipped and took the Lord's Supper together. He would then leave and go to his apartment. I was beyond feeling hurt, embarrassed, ashamed, and just in disbelief.

Meanwhile I continued worshipping and serving faithfully at my church. My church had become my refuge. It was there I felt safe and comfortable. I somehow was able to escape the reality of my life as I worshipped. I prayed that the Holy Spirit would work through sermons and songs to bring the needed transformation in my husband.

Contrary to what was really going on, our actions before man indicated that our marriage was healthy. I felt too ashamed and embarrassed to tell anyone at church or work (at that time) what was going on. So I covered for him, and I covered for myself as well.

As time passed I struggled to maintain the ability to cope at work. The stressful situation had taken a toll on me physically. On two occasions while preparing for work, I fainted, and the paramedics were called. My doctor determined that I needed to take medicine to regulate my stress and blood pressure levels.

At Night

The nighttime was just as unbearable as the daytime. I roamed from room to room, from the bed to the couch, and from the couch to the bed trying to rest. I became all too familiar with **Psalm 6:6 which says, "I am worn out from my groaning. All night I flood my bed with weeping and drench my couch with tears."** During this time my prayer life consisted of sobbing, screaming, and many times blaming God for not stopping my husband from leaving. I would often go into my prayer closet to pray, simply uttering words like, "Help Me, Lord." Somehow, I knew God understood.

Solemn Assembly, January 2011

My husband and I hosted Solemn Assembly (a week-long time of fasting for our church) at our home that year. Other couples came to our home to study the word of God and to fellowship. Our Couple's Ministry Leaders coordinated all the events for the evening with my husband. The Leaders had no idea that my husband was no longer living with me.

That evening, the husband of one of the couples attending shared that he and his wife had experienced some difficulties in their marriage and would like the group to pray for them. Everyone, including my husband, laid hands upon them and prayed for them and their marriage. Once again I was in disbelief that my husband was able to pray and lay hands upon another couple while not mentioning that he had abandoned his wife, and therefore, desired the group to pray for us as well. He didn't say a word and neither did I. I did not uncover what was going on at "our home." After Solemn Assembly ended that night, my husband gathered his things and left our home, and he went back to his apartment.

Godly Counseling, January 2011

I had finally reached my breaking point. The next day, I prayed and cried most of the day. I could not believe that my husband didn't care enough about our marriage to seek prayer and counseling for us. I could no longer allow pride to prevent me from seeking accountability and help for our marriage.

I prayed and sought guidance on what I should do and how I should do it. **James 1:5 says, "If any of you lack wisdom, you should ask God who gives generously to all who ask, and He will not rebuke us for asking."**

I sought counseling with our couple's leaders, an assistant pastor, and finally with the senior pastor at our church. My husband did attend a couple of counseling sessions with me.

After counseling with Dr. Evans, he outlined a plan that, if implemented, would begin a restoration process for our marriage. We both agreed to work the plan that was outlined for us. However, after the first session with Dr. Evans my husband decided he was not going to participate any further in the plan, consequently he no longer attended the counseling sessions. I continued receiving counseling from both Dr. Evans and Pastor Gibson throughout the year.

Divorce 2012

After 20 years of marriage my husband chose to divorce. I did not want a divorce and certainly did not agree with the decision my husband made. He had no biblical reason (s) to seek a divorce.

I experienced countless sleepless nights. I felt hopeless, helpless, embarrassed, ashamed, and my heart ached with pain. I felt emotionally, physically, and spiritually abandoned. The man I had come to love and admire had lacerated my heart and I was bleeding profusely.

I thought he would always have the best interest of our family at heart, that he would protect, cherish, and love me until death do us part.

But he didn't.

Mark 10:7-9 reads, "For this reason a man should leave his father and mother and be united to his wife, and the two shall become one flesh. So they are no longer two, but one. Therefore what God has joined together, let no man separate."

My burden was so heavy, but I knew I couldn't give up on God. Although I had done all I knew to do yet nothing had changed. My response was to still stand!

Stand

- Stand on the promises of God
- Stand while meditating on His words (day and night)
- Stand, trusting that God allowed this pain to grow my faith in Him
- Stand, knowing that God is God, and I am not
- Stand, expecting God to right the wrong

Dr. Charles Stanley, Pastor of the First Baptist Church in Atlanta, Georgia often says, "Obey God and leave all the consequences to Him."

God's desire is to move us from a place of stagnation to a place of transformation in Him. We cannot change ourselves. But the Holy Spirit can transform our hearts and our lives.

God can use what the enemy meant for evil to strategically provide purpose and meaning for the next season in our lives.

Romans 8:28 says, "And we know that God works all things together for the good of those who love Him, and are called according to His purpose."

Sometimes circumstances in our lives seem to go from bad to worse. The enemy wants us to believe God is not with us, that He has forsaken us. This is how the disciples felt when Jesus instructed them to get in the boat so they could cross to the other side of the lake.

Matthew 8:24

Matthew tells the story about Jesus when He told His disciples to get in the boat so they could cross to the other side of the lake. Suddenly a furious storm came.

The volatile winds blew and the water beat hard against their boat. The disciples struggled against the tumultuous winds and the boat was engulfed with the waves as they tried to row. Their situation looked hopeless (in the physical). They feared they would die. To make matters worse, Jesus was asleep on a cushion at the back of the boat. Then, the disciples woke Jesus up. They complained about their situation and were concerned that He didn't care if they died. Because Jesus is omniscient, all knowing, the stormy situation did not surprise Him. Jesus commanded the wind and rain to cease, and they did!

There was no doubt that a fierce storm was raging as the disciples struggled to get to the other side. However, the disciples soon discovered that God was greater than their storm. When storms rage in your life, "Be still and know that He is God" (Psalm 46:10). During your storm fix your eyes on Jesus and trust Him to guide you safely and gently to the other side. God can use stormy situations to grow our faith while revealing that He is the Great I Am.

What Now?

Jeremiah 29:11 says," For I know the plans that I have for you, declares the LORD. Plans to prosper you and not to harm you, plans to give you hope and a future." The Holy Spirit revealed to me that... yes, a traumatic thing had occurred in my life. Yet I (God) am almighty, I am in control, and I have heard every prayer and seen every tear. **Hebrews 4:13 says that NOTHING in all creation is hidden from God's sight. Everything is uncovered and laid bare before the eyes of Him to whom we must give account.**

God had allowed my husband to proceed with his plans in seeking a divorce; however, that didn't mean God approved it.

The Grieving Process

Divorce is profoundly painful. It has a devastating effect on children (regardless of their age), family, friends, neighbors, believers and non-believers. I became intensely angry. I resented the changes it forced upon me and my family. I felt ashamed that we had failed at demonstrating how a Christian couple should work together to ensure a positive outcome in marriage. Fear and anxiety were my constant companions. I couldn't bear to think about what tomorrow would look like. I weaved in and out of depression. Many days I was unable to concentrate, unable to sleep, and unable to eat. There were days when I thought I had healed in certain areas, but something would trigger the hurt and the grieving would start all over again.

I have learned there is no right or wrong way to grieve. The important thing is to allow yourself as much time as you need in order to grieve and to heal. While grieving I meditated on bible verses that spoke specifically to my situation. I read and meditated on them daily; I had several spiritual mothers who stood in prayer with me daily. I stayed connected with other believers at my church. Although sometimes my faith waivered, it did not fail. The following verse was one that gave me reassurance and comfort in God. **Isaiah 41:10, "So do not fear, for I am with you; do not be dismayed, for I am your God; I will strengthen you and help you; I will uphold you with my righteous hand!" AMEN!!**

Connect with Others

Although my story is still developing, I continue to be available to God. I surrendered all the hurt, disappointments, and forgiveness to Him. I gave Him permission to heal me inside and out. My desire is for God to use me to encourage and support other ladies who have experienced similar hurts. I have been tremendously blessed by so many people who have poured into my life during my time of need. God has overwhelmed me with His grace and mercy throughout this difficult season in my life.

In 1 Thessalonians 5:11, we are told to encourage one another and to build up one another. Shortly after the devastating and abrupt end of my marriage, God began placing women in my path that had experienced the same hurt and pain as I had. I became a Small Group Facilitator at my church. The ladies in our group have developed strong and lasting friendships. Connecting with other ladies has kept us from always feeling alone and isolated. We have maintained accountability within our group with weekly phone calls, prayer, and encouragement. When we allow God to use us, He will place specific people in our path who He desires for us to encourage.

My Pastor, Dr. Tony Evans, teaches us that whatever we desire from God, we should be that same thing in the life of another person. If you need encouraging, be an encourager; if you need a shoulder to cry on, allow others to cry on your shoulder.

Choose to Forgive

In addition to connecting with other women, God made it crystal clear that I would not be healed from this tragedy until I learned to forgive His way.

I would love to tell you that this was an easy process for me. However, that is not my story. As previously shared, this had been the most devastating and painful hurt I had ever experienced. Therefore, I knew the Holy Spirit would have to guide me through this stage of healing. With much prayer and guidance, eventually forgiveness became my inner response to all my hurt. I realize that forgiveness didn't minimize, justify, or excuse the wrong that was done.

Forgiveness

- Is not just a feeling
- Is not for the other person, it's for me
- Is not pretending the other person didn't hurt you
- Does not condone what the other person did

Nevertheless, God commands us to forgive.

Forgiveness does mean to release someone from a debt. The debt being the offense that was done to you, then begin praying for that individual. Therefore, I was able to forgive.

Ephesians 4:31-32 reminds us, "Get rid of all bitterness, rage, and anger, brawling and slander, along with every form of malice. Be kind and compassionate to one another, forgiving each other, just as in Christ, God forgave you."

Wait on God

I have to admit, waiting on God for direction has not been an easy process either. This is an area where I needed some refining. God's word says that I should rest in the Lord and wait patiently for him. Waiting on God means there are times when I have to be still and quiet before Him so I can hear what He is saying. Often, it was during those quiet and revered times before God, the enemy confronted me with thoughts, resulting in my feeling low and discouraged. The more the enemy yelled at me, the more God reminded me in His still, quiet voice, "I have not abandoned you, and I will never leave, nor forsake you." I would gratefully lay in God's lap of mercy, grace, and unconditional love. Knowing that He is sovereign, and He is in control of every detail that concerns me gave me peace.

The questions I began asking myself changed from *Will you wait on God* to **how** *will you wait on God?* Will you passively sit around complaining; or will you use your energy to encourage others? I chose the latter.

Sometimes it seems that darkness is overpowering the light; it seems like the enemy is winning, and God is losing. It seems like the game is over, but it's not. As you surrender all your disappointments and hurts to God, He will guide you safely through your storm.

Waiting on God Produces

- Faith and trust in Him
- Perseverance in standing on God's promises
- Transformation in our character
- Confidence that God alone is our source

Now

I am eternally grateful to God for extending His favor, mercy, and grace to my son and me. I am in awe of how God has sustained us through the years. I have been able to focus on healing and growth through Christian-based programs and Bible studies such as Celebrate Recovery, Bible Study Fellowship International (BSF), OCBF Women's Small Group, Free at Last (OCBF) Women of Transformation Ministry, and countless prayers and words of encouragement from my pastors, family, and friends.

If this is your season of hurt and pain, know that God is with you; if you are anxious about tomorrow, know that your life, your security, and your future are all in God's hands.

"For I know the plans I have for you, declares the LORD, plans for welfare and not for calamity; to give you a future and a hope." Jeremiah 29:11.

About Jeannette Dixon

Jeannette Dixon is an educator, facilitator, and a speaker. She has spent more than two decades addressing the academic and social needs of children. Jeannette uses various keys such as motivation, acceptance, communication, modeling, and commitment to God's Word to make a difference in the lives of children and adults.

Jeannette has facilitated Women's Small Group sessions at Oak Cliff Bible Fellowship in Dallas, Texas for the past several years, under the vision and leadership of Dr. Tony Evans. In addition, Jeannette is a member of Women of Transformation Ministry, which is dedicated to guiding women from brokenness to hope and victory in Christ Jesus.

She received her Bachelor's Degree from The University of Southern Mississippi and her Master's Degree in Curriculum and Instruction from Sarasota University. Jeannette has a passion for studying God's Word and seeks to exemplify the qualities of a Kingdom Agenda Woman for her son and others.

Jeannette's focus is on Christian Ministry opportunities as she continues to encourage other women to forgive, love, and rest in Jesus regardless of their circumstances.

TERRI HOGUE

Faith and prayer together are unstoppable.

An Angel Lost, Blessed With Two Miracles

Have you ever noticed most people do not smile when they are at the doctor's office? I never noticed because I rarely had a reason to see the doctor. That all changed in June of 2009. I was still enjoying my honeymoon, nine months married and everything was great. I had met the perfect person for me and we loved our life together.

From the moment we were married, we had been trying to conceive. Some of you may be thinking, Why the rush? You had only been married nine months. Well, there's this thing called AGE that creeps up on you. At the time I was 39 and Greg was 49, we weren't getting any younger. Hence, the clock was ticking! We were both worried that if we waited any longer our kid(s) would be taking care of us when they were teenagers instead of us taking care of them! I didn't want to waste time, especially since Greg had a change of heart about having kids.

When I met Greg he told me that he didn't want to have kids. All three of his brothers had kids and to him fatherhood looked too hard; he just wanted to be the "fun" uncle. I remember telling him that not having kids was a deal-breaker for me. I had always wanted to have four kids, but as I got older I realized four was probably not going to happen but maybe one or two were still possible.

Over the course of the next four months I would run into Greg at different events through mutual friends. We had great conversations and the more time I spent with him the more I was drawn to him. He was a gentle soul with a very loving heart. When we finally went on an official first date, I remember thinking I probably shouldn't go out with him because he doesn't want to have kids, but I went anyway. I'm so glad I did!

As you get older, you tend to learn things. One of the things I learned was that you can't change a person nor should you try because more than likely they will revert to their natural ways.

After about three months of dating, I realized that Greg was a keeper. It just so happened that I had planned a trip to Italy with one of my besties and her mom. I looked at the trip as good timing in that the time apart would allow me to see if I really missed Greg. My girlfriend's mom told us that every time we visited a different church in Italy we should light a candle and say the same prayer(s) in each church. She said if we did God would answer our prayer(s). I said the same two prayers in all 17 churches we visited, including the Vatican. Not only did I pray those two prayers in Italy, but I prayed them in every church that I visited after our trip. The first prayer was answered the day we got married. Faith and prayer together are unstoppable.

After a lot of thinking and praying I decided that having Greg in my life was more important to me than having kids. I couldn't imagine my life without him. If it meant not having kids, then I was ok with that so long as we were together.

When I told Greg, he was shocked and surprised. He proceeded to tell me that he had been doing a lot of thinking too. He realized that he couldn't ask me to give up something that he knew I wanted. Now I was in shock! *Did I just hear him right, he wants to have a child?* Wow, I wasn't expecting that. *Is he just telling me what I want to hear or is he committed to having a child?*

In my very "Terri" fashion I said to Greg, "Just to be clear, if we do this you are all in, right?" And by all in I meant we are both 100% committed to being parents, dirty diapers and all. I even went so far as to tell him, "Don't do me any favors, because I do not want to be a single married parent.

He said, "Yes. I am all in." I sat in the living room with a big smile on my face. One thing I have always admired about Greg is his ability to keep his word. I knew when he told me he was all in, he meant it. Prayer number two had been answered. Faith and prayer together are unstoppable.

When I went to get my annual physical, I mentioned to my doctor that Greg and I had been trying to have a baby for about nine months. She immediately asked me to remind her how old I was.

I said, "Thirty-eight."

She then told me it's not uncommon for women over 35 to need some extra help in getting pregnant. *Extra help...what does she mean by that?* She then went on to educate me on the subject of infertility. I have to admit my knowledge on infertility was minimal. She referred me to an infertility doctor that she had used to conceive. She mentioned he had a team of good doctors and they get all their patients pregnant. After my doctor's appointment, I researched infertility.

I shared what my doctor told me with Greg and he said I should make an appointment so we could find out what the next steps were. In June of 2009 we had our first appointment with our doctor. She was very positive, honest, and explained treatment options to us. She definitely made me feel better because she shared that she had helped women in their 40's get pregnant. Our journey began; little did we know that our journey would last three years.

Even though our doctor explained everything very well, I don't think we quite grasped what was ahead of us. It started with a series of appointments for everything from blood work to monitoring my cycle to determine how many follicles I produced every month. A follicle is a fluid-filled sac that contains an immature egg. Follicles are found in the ovaries. Follicle growth and development are tracked during fertility treatments. Greg also had to get tested, but he passed with flying colors.

The issue was with me.

Attempt number one was to have me take medicine which would force me to ovulate because I wasn't producing follicles on my own. I happily took the medicine and we quickly realized that I was going to need something stronger than a couple of pills. Before we started working on treatment number two, my doctor decided to make sure I was not suffering from a tubal blockage. She performed a Hysterosalpingogram (HSG) procedure. The test shows whether the fallopian tubes are open or blocked and whether a blockage is at the junction of the tube and uterus or at the other end of the tube. She injected some dye into my uterine cavity, which I have to admit was somewhat painful and it was through that procedure that we learned I had a polyp. My doctor successfully removed the polyp through an out-patient procedure.

We were now ready to move to a different treatment option, Intrauterine Insemination (IUI). At this point we had been seeing the doctor for six months—two, sometimes three times a week. It was during the frequent visits I started noticing that no one in the waiting room smiled or spoke to each other. I always felt a little odd because Greg and I would get there eager to see what the next step was but then we would walk in and conform to the mood at hand.

It wasn't until much later that I began to understand what some of the women in the waiting room were going through. No wonder they weren't smiling or quick to say hello. They had probably been undergoing treatments for a lot longer than I had.

The IUI procedure was different in that I didn't need to take a pill; instead, I had to inject myself with a shot at the same time every day for a specified number of days. When the doctor told me I was going to have to give myself a shot, I wanted to say, *No, never mind, I don't want to do this.* At one point I even asked if I could come into the office every day and have one of the nurses give me the shot. For a fee I could, but then I did the math and quickly realized that I just needed to put my big girl pants on and suck it up and inject myself. The nurses at the doctor's office were really nice and showed me how to properly give myself a shot in my thigh.

Here's where the procedures also started to get expensive. The medicine that I needed was not something that I could pick up at a pharmacy. It had to be special-ordered through my insurance company and shipped overnight. There was also a timing element involved in that I needed to start the injections on a specific day to align with my ovarian cycle.

For the most part, dealing with the insurance company wasn't too difficult. I always managed to get my medicine in time. Prior to starting our infertility journey the doctor's office had informed me that my insurance would cover half of most treatment costs and medication. According to the doctor's office, I had great coverage because they had seen other insurance companies that didn't cover infertility treatments. I had to remind myself of that every time I called to order my medication because our financial responsibility for each round of treatments was between $3,000 - $3,500 dollars. Each round of treatments was between 10 -14 days. When I told Greg he said, "It's ok, we will find a way and it will all be worth it in the end."

It took me about 30 minutes to pump myself up to dispense that first injection. It actually didn't hurt as much as I thought it would. Little did I know I would become an expert at giving myself shots. I did exactly what the doctor said to do and with the help of the medicine I had produced five follicles! The IUI procedure was painless and quick. In nine days I would go back for a blood draw to see if I was pregnant. It just so happened that the blood draw fell on a

Sunday morning. We went in first thing and then went to church.

When we got out of church I had a message from the doctor. We listened to the message in the parking lot at church, the test was positive, we were pregnant! We were excited and couldn't wait for our next doctor's appointment.

Two or three weeks passed before we went to the doctor. We saw the gestational sac but didn't hear a heartbeat. Our doctor told us it might be a day or two early to detect the heartbeat and asked us to come back in two weeks. We had no reason to believe anything was wrong so when we went back to the doctor's we were heartbroken to learn there was no heartbeat and a miscarriage was inevitable. My doctor referred to it as a blighted ovum miscarriage. She recommended I have a Dilation & Curettage (D&C) procedure. I'm not sure how but we both held back the tears in the doctor's office until we got to the car. I now understood even more why the women in the waiting room didn't smile or want to chat.

On the day of the D&C procedure, we were ushered to a different waiting area; one that we didn't know existed. While we were waiting for them to come and get me we started talking to a man who was waiting for his wife. He told us they had been trying for a while to have a baby and the first time they got pregnant his wife miscarried at five months. All of a sudden my situation didn't seem so bad. I couldn't imagine how he and his wife had dealt with a miscarriage at five months. At this point I was eight weeks. I think the story he shared helped me get through the next few weeks. Every time I would start to feel sorry for myself I was reminded of his story and how that could have been us. We had lost our angel, which we found out later was a boy.

Through science and technology our doctor shared with us the reason I miscarried was because I had an extra 10th chromosome. Even if I had carried our son to full term he wouldn't have lived very long. I was grateful to learn "why" I had suffered a miscarriage. It helped me to continue to move forward in our journey to becoming parents.

Up to this point, we hadn't told anyone in our families that we were trying to have a baby. I think everyone figured since we were both older and set in our ways that we probably would forego having kids. I had shared what we were going through with two of my besties who had been very supportive. When we finally told everyone after the

D&C procedure what we had been going through, our support system grew extensively.

We had prayer warriors everywhere, which we deeply appreciated. It was then I realized that we had committed the great "infertility taboo"—talking about it openly with others. I didn't know it at the time but in the beginning I think I was a little embarrassed about being infertile. I think it was because I didn't know any other women personally who were struggling like me. The truth of the matter was that when I did confide in my two besties as to what we were going through, I felt better about our situation and myself.

Dealing with infertility is not easy and can cause a strain on your marriage if you let it. The frequent doctor's appointments, injections, unsuccessful attempts and planned sex can be very draining on a couple. For those of you who are struggling with infertility, I highly suggest you find more than one support system, separate ones if need be. Talking to each other and others will help. Faith and prayer always help. My husband and I seemed to grow a little closer each time we went through a procedure.

After the miscarriage, we waited about two months before we went back to the doctor to discuss next steps. Since we had success with the IUI procedure she suggested we try the IUI procedure again. We attempted the IUI procedure two more times with no success. At this point we had spent a couple of years trying to get pregnant. It was time to take a more aggressive approach.

We moved on to In Vitro Fertilization (IVF). I was over 40 so the odds weren't exactly in my favor. I had about a 20% chance of IVF working. Once again we did everything the doctor told us. Greg was more involved with the preparation for the IVF procedure because he had to give me the injections in my hip. This was really hard on him because he felt like he was hurting me but he wasn't. I had gotten used to the shots.

We attempted IVF twice with no success. After I got off the phone with the nurse who informed me that the second IVF procedure had not worked I told my husband I was done. I had always considered myself to be a very strong woman but I was emotionally drained. I was tired of crying and being told, "I'm sorry but the pregnancy test was negative. Please call and schedule an appointment with the doctor when you are ready."

I asked my husband, "We have so much love to give. Why isn't God blessing us with a child?"

He hugged me and replied, "I don't know."

Over the next couple of months we researched adoption. Our age was a factor and in some cases an immediate denial. Besides, it could take years to adopt. We gave up on that option pretty quickly.

About four or five months passed and we went to visit my family. There had been two babies born in my family over the course of six months and I was eager to see the babies. When we returned home my husband said, "I think we should try again."

I looked at him and said, "Try what again?"

He said, "I think we should try one more time to have a baby."

I immediately said, "No. I don't have it in me to try again."

He looked at me and said, "I saw you rocking Julius to sleep. You looked so happy and comfortable. We need to try again."

I have to admit I was really surprised my husband wanted us to try again; after all, he initially didn't want to have kids. I told him, "No, I just can't go through the disappointment again, it will break me."

He said, "Will you at least make an appointment with the doctor to see what other options we might have?"

I wanted to say no again, but then I reminded myself that my husband rarely asks for anything; the least I could do was make the appointment. Deep down inside I had already made up my mind that there were no more options that I wanted to try.

On the day of the appointment we went in and sadly nothing had changed in the waiting room other than now I wasn't smiling or talking. I had become just like everyone else and I didn't expect my outcome to change for the better.

We visited with the doctor and she discussed three options with us. The first was IVF, which we were well versed on. The difference this time is that my doctor would have me take the strongest medication possible along with the maximum dosage possible to increase the probability of producing more viable follicles.

The second option was to use a surrogate. Cost was a huge factor in that our insurance didn't cover this option. We would need about 25K to get started. We had already spent close to 20k on IUI and IVF treatments. This was the least favorite option.

The last option was embryo adoption. We had never heard of adopting an embryo. Our doctor explained that embryo adoption was a new way to adopt. Rather than adopting a child through the normal channels, embryo adoption allows the female in the adopting family to carry and deliver the baby. She further explained that sometimes when couples undergo IVF treatment, there are more embryos created than actually used, thus embryos remain available. It's up to the couple if they want to discard the embryos or put them up for adoption. If we decided to go with this option, we would be provided with a list of viable embryos. The list would include information such as donor ages, ethnicity, eye and hair color, education, weight, height, and medical background.

Over the next couple of weeks, my husband and I did some research on embryo adoption. It was very interesting to us and not much different than adopting a child except that the woman gets to experience pregnancy and childbirth.

According to embryoadoption.org, there are over 600,000 viable embryos in the United States waiting to be adopted. That's a lot of babies waiting to be born. If you are struggling and feel like you have run out of options, you haven't; please research embryo adoption or talk to your infertility doctor about that option. The cost is comparable to IVF.

We were very torn between IVF and embryo adoption. Since we were familiar with IVF, we decided to try IVF one more time.

Prior to starting the treatments, I went to see my Reverend and confessed my anger and feelings about God not allowing or blessing me to have children. I told him how angry and broken I was about losing my son so soon after conceiving. We had so much love to give and I knew we would make great parents. I mentioned how hard it was to be happy for friends, family members and women in general who were giving birth. It was really difficult to hold back the tears when I was around a baby.

He asked me questions about my prayer life and how I was expressing myself and I answered. I shared that I was praying every prayer I knew how to pray. He then shared with me that I needed to be bold when I pray, calling out exactly what I wanted/needed from God. I left his office and followed his instructions.

It was two days after Christmas and both my husband and I were on vacation. We went in early to have the pregnancy test done and then decided to go see the ice sculpture at the Gaylord Hotel. It was almost noon when we left the Gaylord. My husband asked me if I checked my phone to see if the doctor had called. It was then I realized I had left my cell phone at home!

That was the first time I can remember ever forgetting my cell phone. I think a part of me was trying to avoid the phone call because I was so used to receiving disappointing news. When we got home I had a message. I looked at my husband and said I don't feel different. I feel exactly like I have each time we have tried. I played the message on speaker phone and we listened as the nurse said your HCG level was 80. "You're pregnant. Please call and make an appointment to see your doctor in two weeks."

We both looked at each other in complete shock. *Really? I'm pregnant? Is that what she said?* My HCG level was a lot higher than the first pregnancy, which made me feel good. Faith and prayer together are unstoppable.

Over the next couple of weeks, we didn't talk very much about the pregnancy. I think we were both scared that the same thing was going to happen all over again.

We went to our appointment and my doctor told me my HCG level was great. "Let's see how everything looks," she said.

I took a deep breath and said a quick prayer as I lay back on the table and the doctor started the sonogram.

She shrieked, "Look! It's twins!" and then we heard their strong heartbeats!

I looked over at my husband and he had a little tear streaming down his face. I, on the other hand, was smiling from ear to ear and thinking, *Wow, my prayers were answered. I'm going to be a mommy; we have been blessed with two miracles.*

I couldn't have asked for a better pregnancy. I never experienced any morning sickness or weird cravings. The worse part was the occasional leg cramps and carpal tunnel in both hands. Since I was 42, the pregnancy was considered high risk. I saw my doctor and my babies every three weeks. I gained 37 pounds and delivered Samuel and Sofia by C-section when I was 37 weeks on August 13, 2012. They are a true blessing and our miracles.

I thank God every day for my husband. He is good to me. I never thought I could love my husband more than the day we were married, but I do. He is an amazing father and so patient with Samuel and Sofia. He's changed more dirty diapers and cleaned up more sickness than I have. Not bad for someone who thought he didn't want to be a father. Greg now tells me that being a daddy is the best thing ever. The three years of doctor visits, disappointment, tears, frustration, anger and expenses were worth it.

Infertility is not easy to deal with. Here's what I would do differently if I'd known then what I know now:

- I would talk to people who have been down the infertility journey and ask them to be brutally honest about their experiences. It's important to hear the good, bad and ugly.
- I would lean on family and friends more and find a support group.

- I would research the costs associated with infertility, as well as other options, such as adoption upfront and determine a financial threshold.

- Most importantly, have a plan on how to not let infertility destroy your marriage. Greg and I were lucky in that it brought us closer together but that's not always the case.

- Fully understand the journey you are about to start and together make a commitment on what works for both of you.

About Terri Hogue

Terri Hogue is a native Texan. She grew up in San Angelo and now lives in Plano, Texas. She earned her Bachelor's degree in Communication and Business Administration and a Master's Degree in Organizational Management. Terri is married to Greg, her best friend and without his support none of this would be possible. Although their struggles with infertility were at times heartbreaking and emotionally draining, she and Greg were blessed with two miracles, Samuel Joel and Sofia Giselle on August 13, 2012. Terri can be reached via email at hoguetwins13@gmail.com.

SONJA JONES

"Death is swallowed up in victory."

"O death, where is your victory?

O death, where is your sting?"

– 1 Cor. 15:53-55 (NLT)

The Last Sunday Morning

This story is dedicated to my mother, Mary Louise Gibson, who raised me with love, and care and supported me with prayers and wisdom. And to my heartbeats, my nieces, Nyla and Gabrielle, who inspire me daily to be better than the day before. You are loved and valued beyond measure!!

I barely breathed as I walked down the wide hallway, with its floors buffed to a new nickel shine. I walked swiftly past half-opened doors, glancing hesitantly into rooms with beds, each one contained a patient with eyes vacant and pleading for comfort and voices likely worn thin and raspy from tubes, medications and lack of use. Hospitals have *never* been my thing, but this was an unavoidable exception. I was heading to see my grandmother, Hazel B. Gibson, whom I affectionately called Gramms. I needed to kiss her face and feel her loving arms around me and bask in her presence for a bit. My need to see her was purely selfish; I wanted this as much for her as myself, but much more for myself.

This visit was long overdue. I live in the Dallas/Fort Worth area and had been unable to make the long drive home to the rustic bayou of Gibson, Louisiana for quite some time due to work and personal obligations. Prior to my drive on this chilly November morning, thoughts of my Gramms were mingled with quick, yet fervently whispered prayers that God would, *"Just please let me see her again...please!"*

For months, whenever Gramms and I would get the chance to speak by phone, she didn't always have a lot to say...illness can do that to a person. She tired easily these days, but she loved for me to reminisce about things from my childhood or sing her a "spiritual," referring to old Baptist hymns.

Sometimes, if I listened carefully, I could hear her sweet voice join mine for a verse of "This Little Light of Mine, I'm Going to Let It Shine." In that way, we closed the miles between us and cemented our connection.

My Gramms had dozens of grandchildren, and it would be easy to get a bit lost in the shuffle, but not with her. She had a way of making each of us feel loved, valued and cared for…it's a gift…just as her life was a gift, a living testimony to each of us who loved and cherished her.

For the previous two years, I had been acutely aware that she wasn't as strong as she used to be. Things were changing and like it or not, I was going to have to face some certainties in what would likely be the not so distant future. The shadow of death was a present, but unspoken reality that loomed all too close for comfort.

While that type of thing could not be adequately conveyed over the phone during weekly conversations with my mom, I could tell that things were different. Sometimes—who am I kidding?—*most* times, even when I wouldn't say anything about it, I noticed her change in tone when I asked about Gramms. I desperately tried to ignore the sudden drop in volume…her voice barely above a whisper, as she relayed the latest updates. I could hear the fear and desperation in her voice, and through the phone, my mind's eye could feel the weight of the sadness that draped over her hunched shoulders like a worn, wet blanket. It was the heavy sound of imminent heartbreak that I heard in her, that unfortunately, I could not bear to acknowledge for fear it would take me over the edge with my emotions. There I was, hundreds of miles away, my Gramms in ill health, and my mom, her oldest daughter, was on the phone trying to hold it together. Faced with those overwhelming circumstances, my outward bravado failed and I was left speechless. Nothing to say, and absolutely nothing I could do. After all, I am *her* oldest daughter and nothing within me can prepare me for someday being in this position myself.

Death is a certainty for all of us, but losing anyone you care for is a challenge…an ordeal that none of us ever wants to face. Though I believe that for my mom, my grandmother's oldest daughter, the pain may have been a bit more acute. My mother mourned the mere *thought* of losing Gramms long before she was actually gone. I could sympathize from the standpoint of how I would feel if something were to happen to her. But until you experience it for yourself, you cannot begin to understand the pain and anguish of losing a parent, especially your mother. From the moment you are created in the womb, the two of you are connected long before you take that first breath. In my heart, it is a connection second only to that with our Almighty Father God. To have to watch the steady decline of the one you hold most dear, knowing the end result has to be maddening for those left behind.

Gramms had been ill for years with a myriad of illnesses that came from aging after having worked hard all her life beside my grandfather, Lawless Sr., to raise their huge family of twelve sons and daughters. They were not farmers, but they literally worked the land to put food on the table and I can honestly say that while there may have been lean days, there were few, if any, hungry days, at least by the time I came along. I knew that she was pretty bad off, but I had no real clue just how bad things really were. My mother would always whisk away the bulk of my concerns in a calm, soothing voice, telling me that Gramms was in good hands. Yet, Gramms's trips to the hospital became more frequent and lengthy. Try as she might, Mom's attempts did little to soothe me. All I could do, all any of us could do, was pray.

Early one weekday morning as I was preparing to go to work, a call came from my mom. She was clearly exhausted, having spent the night in a chair beside my grandmother's hospital bed. I had done it before myself countless times so I knew that she had not gotten an adequate amount of rest. It's hard to rest in the hospital as a patient...constantly being poked, prodded and checked on, but let me tell you, being the family member who keeps watch, is not easy either. There is no comfort, physically or emotionally, as all you can do is stand there watching the parade of nurses and doctors go in and out all night long. She was not asking me to come home, but rather, in her exhaustion, she just wept quietly. Through her tears, she spoke not of my grandmother, but of the calls, cards and flowers from those near and far and the visitors who had stopped by to offer a word of comfort during an impossibly difficult time. We spoke of family who had called to say that they were on the way to likely say a goodbye that no one welcomes. I didn't need for her to say the words. Before we ended the call I had already begun to make plans in my head to drive home to the bayou before the end of the week.

I continued a bit further down the hallway, anxious, but not in a hurry. When I arrived at her door, I hesitated only a moment before entering. I was met with greetings from various family members who filled every possible nook and cranny of the room. My mom and my Aunt Ella hovered around the bed like guardian angels, combing her hair and attending patiently to her every need. My Uncle Cookie sat quietly, his face set like a flint, exhibiting a quiet strength that somehow offered a measure of comfort despite our heavy hearts. I knew that he was hurting, but for him to break at this moment, would likely have broken us all.

Amid the greetings, the room still felt somber and serious, drenched in a reluctant sadness. My grandmother's eyes were on me. She was smiling slightly. She looked so frail and helpless in that bed. Her once beautiful skin now appeared sallow, and eyes that used to dance with joy, were sunken and lifeless. The sight of her appearance alone caused my heart to skip a beat.

As I bent to put my arms across her,—I knew that she recognized me, but I could only feel the whisper of her breath against my face even as my ears were met with silence. I saw her lips moving, but Gramms had lost the ability to speak. I looked up into my mothers' eyes and without a word, her expression confirmed what my heart now knew: Gramms had had a stroke. It was unlikely that any of us would ever hear her voice again.

Dozens of images…memories of time spent with my grandmother began to flow through my head. For as long as

I can remember, Sunday mornings began on Saturday evening. Hair was pressed and curled, clothes ironed and laid out nicely and Sunday dinner already made or extremely close to it, along with a peach cobbler with a perfect lattice crust well-covered and hidden out of reach of those who would rather not wait until dessert time. Nothing left but to put the cornbread in the oven as soon as we walked into the door from church. It was the ritual of our family to prepare for Sunday morning service on Saturday and Gramms had everybody in check. Faith, family and good food were the most important things to her.

My passion for cooking is certainly a part of her legacy to me. I absolutely *love* to cook and own enough cook wear to furnish a small restaurant. My Gramms used to say that nothing in the world said welcome home like the smell of good food when you walk into the door. I know that I carry that belief within me because I've spent so much time cooking for those I love and care for. I still pray before I put the first ingredients together...something I saw her do on countless occasions. She would bless her own hands as they prepared the food. That speaks volumes to me about the love she had for nurturing her family.

When it came time for church, I recall running through the house as a small child trying to find as many things as possible to fill my little black patent leather purse. You couldn't tell me that I wasn't grown up with a purse to carry even if it was only filled with peppermints, tissues and maybe a couple of quarters to put in Sunday school and church. I needed something to occupy my time and attention without getting me into trouble during service.

My circle of cousins, my brother, Marvin and I were good kids, but full of mischief, so Gramms kept a watchful eye on all of us, even as we sat in service. If any one or all of us stepped out of line, Gramms would peer down from her perch in the Senior Choir and give a look over those thick little glasses that pretty much scared us straight....at least for a bit. That one look said it all! We were loved, but Gramms didn't play. If I received that look, I *knew* that I was in trouble and for the remainder of the service, I sat with my back against the pew giving rapt attention to the preacher like I actually understood what he was shouting about.

I don't know what was worse, wondering (slightly certain) that I was going to "get it" when I got home or being tapped on the shoulder and taken out during service. Neither was a good look for me. Gramms would take me behind the church and wear me out!!

You can't understand the magnitude of being spanked, well, whupped at church. There must be a rule somewhere that a church beating has to hurt a little bit more, after all, you've "sinned" on the Sabbath. No matter what I said or did, all the prayers in the world couldn't stop her from slipping off that good church shoe and peppering my bottom and legs with swift, firm swats. She would dare me to cry, and even though this little episode was taking place in the spooky cemetery behind the church, I managed not to cry, because as much as I feared Gramms and her shoe, at that moment, I feared the dead people more. Afterwards, I was marched back to church with a stern warning and a much better attitude.

I can laugh about that now…but this Sunday morning was different. Instead of getting ready for service, I was sitting in a chair beside my grandmother's bed, watching her leave and wondering how in the world our family could possibly live without her. This was unchartered territory for all of us. Does life really go on when the one who brought so much love and life to the family is gone?

For all the things and situations we may try our best to prepare for…this was different…this was *Mama*. In my heart I always felt that to lose her, was the end of an era and nothing would ever be the same again. Somehow, in my head, I felt that without her, the world would no longer have any color.

When the last family members had finally departed the evening before, their whispered I love you's and I'll see you tomorrow's continued to linger in the air like smoke. My mom, aunts and uncles were the very last to go and even then, they did so reluctantly. Whenever Gramms was in the hospital, someone from the family always spent the night just to ensure her well-being, but also for our own peace of mind. Tonight was my night with her, but I had no way of knowing, even as family departed, that she was on her way home.

Once the room had cleared, I raised the blanket that covered her body and laid myself alongside her on the bed. I rested my head gently against her shoulder and softly stroked her arm. She stirred just enough to make me feel that this contact was sorely missed. Out of my heart flowed an abundance of love and gratitude and respect for this dear woman. I looked down at her sleeping peacefully, her breathing labored, though assisted by the oxygen tank nearby. I heard my own voice whisper my goodbyes and thank her for loving me well into my adulthood. Not everyone gets to say goodbye and I'm so blessed and honored that God would choose me to hold her hand as she slipped into eternity to meet her King.

Until that second, for every moment of my life, she had been there encouraging, supporting, loving me and praying non-stop and without judgment. That sense of security and unconditional love was significantly diminished with her passing.

For a few minutes, I held my eyes tightly shut. I didn't want to let go just yet. I lay there pressed against her allowing us just to be grandmother and granddaughter for a few minutes longer. There was no crying, no sting of death, just the sound of the oxygen machine and my singular heart beating a steady rhythm I sorely wished could sustain us both.

Try as we might, there is simply no way to prepare for death, even in knowing that someone is about to leave. What I have come to know and understand with her passing is that death is not *our* business or concern, but God's. It is His to decide and ours to accept. Our lives instead should be intertwined with life and living. My Gramms lived a good life. Hazel Beatrice Coleman Gibson lived her life with a purpose, loving her God and her family and affirming her faith by being a living, breathing testimony of the power of the risen Savior! She taught me courage and hope and instilled in me a faith that has carried me through many obstacles. In the end, I know for certain that she welcomed death as a sweet communion with God rather than something to be feared.

Someone once said, "Death is not the greatest loss in life. The greatest loss is what dies inside us while we live." I miss her with all my heart, but any sadness I may feel is overshadowed by the love and legacy she left behind. I miss her, but I do not mourn her; rather, I celebrate the life, the beauty, the essence that was her...my Gramms. Goodnight, Sweet Prince(ss), and flights of angels sing thee to thy rest.

About Sonja Jones

Sonja Jones has long had a love affair with the written word. Growing up in Gibson, Lousiana, she often stayed up past midnight to read the works of notables such as Richard Wright, Maya Angelou and Alice Walker. Inspired by such greats, and gifted with a vivid imagination, she found joy in writing short stories and poetry for her own enjoyment.

Prior to relocating to Texas, she lived in Milwaukee enjoying successes within the non-profit arena and dabbling a bit at stand-up comedy. The desire and passion to write lay dormant within her, until an educational opportunity arose to join a writing workshop at Columbia University in New York City. While there, she fully immersed herself into stirring the creative juices and gained a measure of the discipline truly needed to write consistently.

When not writing, Sonja enjoys reading, working out, cooking and baking. She is also a proud educator within the Texas School System. This is her debut publication, but certainly not her last. She can be reached at SoJoAuthor@yahoo.com

THEREFORE; *Forgive. Love. and. Rest*

VERONICA JONES

"When your words came, I ate them;

they were my joy and heart's delight,

for I bear your name,

Lord, God Almighty."

Jeremiah 15:6

I Forgave, Now What?

I vividly remember speed-racing on my bike with my neighborhood buddies after school one day. As we were barreling from my house to my neighbor's house, which was two doors down, my foot lost placement of the pedal and caused me to literally flip and slide on the rough concrete. I didn't really know what happened until I looked around and then at myself. Next thing I know, I had blood gushing from my left Achilles heel and scrapes on my elbows. Although those wounds had me crying, in pain, and stung really bad, they eventually healed. Likewise, the injuries others might have inflicted upon you might sting, puncture, and leave open wounds, but that doesn't mean you have to let the wounds stay open; they can heal with God's help.

Scars are only a reminder of what we've come from—they don't have to be a continual source of pain. It's difficult to move forward when you're so stuck on what someone has done to you in the past. It's difficult when close family members, friends, spouses, or anyone *period* has hurt you. Forgive. God continuously forgives us; therefore, we are to forgive others.

Vengeance Isn't Key

Vengeance is never key. An eye for an eye, and a tooth for a tooth will leave you blind and with a mouth full of gums. It can destroy you. Even if the other person hasn't apologized, you are to forgive, forget, pray and love them. In this reading experience you'll indulge in the beauty of forgiveness with what it is, how it works, and how to experience it. But remember, you have to do your part and God will handle the rest. Don't be so consumed with holding grudges that you miss out on God's blessings for your life. Or so consumed with holding onto hurt committed towards you that you remain stuck in the past that God wants to release you from. The Bible tells us to "pray for those that persecute you." (Matthew 5:44).

1. Admitting the need for it. (Mark 1:5)

    When you attend an Alcoholics Anonymous meeting the first thing they have you do is admit what you've done. Why is it that verbally admitting your wrong is the first step towards a breakthrough in your stronghold? Spiritually, it's the start of a new way to relate to God. The first step is acknowledgement, because you recognize your situation and you take ownership of your condition. It's as if the opening of your mouth is the key that unlocks your mind and heart to be receptive to what you've admitted. You have to admit that you need forgiveness before accepting it.

2. Forgive Others (Luke 11:4)

God so graciously died for our sins and each time we ask forgiveness of Him, He doesn't think twice about it! Believe it or not, forgiveness is essential to our relationship with Christ as well as our earthly relationships. And even those who have wronged us, should be forgiven also. I'm pretty sure you've been wronged, but I'm also pretty sure that you can't cast the first stone. Consider this: What if God stopped forgiving you? I'm going to stop typing right here. I'm kidding. I have to continue writing because it only gets better from here. Which leads me to point number three.

3. God won't forgive those who don't forgive others
    (Matthew 6:14-15). I love so many things about God,
    but one of those things I love about Him is just how
    forgiving He truly is. I posed the question in my
    previous point (#2), what if God stopped forgiving
    you? It says in His Word "If you forgive those who
    sin against you, your heavenly Father will forgive
    you. If you refuse to forgive others, your Father will
    not forgive your sins." I don't know about you, but I
    would be quite fearful of my life. When you don't
    forgive others, you are actually blocking your own
    blessings God has for you. You are then replacing
    selflessness with self-"flesh"-ness; allowing flesh to
    get in the way of actually releasing that person. You
    are also distancing yourself from the most important
    one, God. Are you going to allow the wrong of one
    person to keep you stuttering in your past? Are you
    going to allow it to keep you from standing in God's
    forgiving grace?

4.   Remembering God's Love

Oftentimes we think we know God's love, but sometimes I honestly think we forget how to show and apply His love. His love should be shown and visually displayed.

Forgiveness is a part of God's love. Remember the scripture given in John 3:16? *For God so loved the world that He gave His only begotten Son; that whosoever believeth in Him shall not perish, but have everlasting life.* Well, God loves the world so much that He gave His only Son, Jesus, to show us what love and compassion look like. He gave His only Son to die for our transgression. He gave His Son as a living example so that when we do mess up, we can seek forgiveness for our wrongs. God loves us enough to forgive us, not merely for our sins, but because of His continuous mercies, which He so graciously and might I mention, repeatedly offers to us. The thought that explodes my mind is that He forgives and then He forgets. (Micah 7:18-19). *Wow,* right? He doesn't hold grudges. He doesn't bring up your past in your face. He doesn't store your sins on a shelf in the back of His mind, but He simply forgets it as if nothing ever happened. How awesome and refreshing to know that you get to start brand new! You get to become a new creature in Christ after you've sought forgiveness. You get to start afresh, I say that to show you that God forgives, and He forgets.

What about you? You have to remember what God has done for you when you're in an "I need to forgive someone" situation. Since God has forgiven you so many times, will it hurt you to forgive someone else? If your answer is yes, then you need to take a deeper look within yourself and pray that God removes the wall that is standing between you and the idea of forgiveness. Colossians 3:13 reads, *Forbearing one another, and forgiving one another, if any man have a quarrel against any: even as Christ forgave you, so also do ye...*

The Word tells us to cast all cares on Him (1 Peter 5:7, *Casting all your care upon him; for he careth for you*). We should also allow God to worry about our wrongs. Remember to be like Christ, to become one with Christ we have to live the way He lived (Ephesians 4:32).

You ever find yourself verbally claiming to forgive a person, but once you and the other individual are around each other, you notice a slight shift in your attitude towards that person? Almost feeling the silent "I still don't like you, but we cool" tension between the two of you. In situations like those, if you've ever been in any, they can be pretty hard to be around. But what I love most about these tense situations, and all situations to be clear, is the lesson I learn, the joy I receive knowing that I've matured, and being able to share my experience.

I was in a situation like that once where an old friend of mine used my name in a false matter, which I was around, but not actually a part of, that caused me to get into trouble with my parents and her parents as well. It took time for me to actually forgive her because I considered her to be one of my close friends, someone who I shared my deepest secrets with. I didn't forgive her the next day I saw her, and it didn't happen the next week. It took time and healing because she was close to my heart. Eventually, I forgave her. It wasn't easy, but I quickly learned that not everyone can be fully trusted, even if they claim to be your friend.

If you truly know me, you are aware that I can be my own worst critic and whether I have to forgive someone or vice versa, I tend to linger in the situation. The only way I'm able to actually overcome is to simply stop worrying about it and give it all to God. Easier said than done, right? Yea, I know, but as I've grown in my walk with Christ, I've had to give it to God; otherwise, it's difficult for me to move forward in life.

Learning to release an unforgiving energy allowed God the opportunity to continue working on my behalf. It created room for Him to continue molding and sculpting me. I've never felt so refreshed and proud that I was able, with God's help, to forgive, forget, release and move forward. What a great feeling to have!

Something we should never forget is the day Jesus was hung on the cross and nearing His death. He said some of the most powerful words with authoritative meaning a man could ever just *think* to say at such a time. Luke 23:34 reads, *Then said Jesus, Father, forgive them; for they know not what they do. And they parted his raiment, and cast lots.* Wow, right? I know, it's so beautiful that He even thought about the people who were crucifying Him, asking God to forgive them of their faults. I often think about how considerate Jesus was to carry His cross and die for my own sins, our sins. We are so undeserving of everything He has to offer to us, yet and still He covers us with His grace, mercy, love, kindness, and so much more. Receiving all of those different types of affections makes me feel honored and privileged. It makes me think: If Jesus can be crucified and still ask God to forgive us, why is it so hard for us to forgive?

One thing we shouldn't do is go to bed holding grudges or being angry with a person. The Bible even shares with us in Ephesians 4:26-27, *Be ye angry, and sin not: let not the sun go down upon your wrath: Neither give place to the devil.* Although it talks about anger, we can relate it to forgiveness as well. We can't allow a negative persistent emotion of unwillingness to forgive to keep us bound from being set free in Christ. Just think…each lash of the whip He took. Each thorn that crowned His head. Each footstep He took closer to His death. Every brass nail that was punctured into his flesh. Every pierce to His side. And every force it took to penetrate the nails using the hammer. It was all with US in mind. It was the sin that He was taking for us so that we could be forgiven and become new in Him.

What Forgiveness Does:

An Eye for an Eye

You ever say to yourself, "I'll forgive them when they come asking for forgiveness?" Or, "I'll forgive when they finally admit they are wrong or come begging on bended knee?" What if they don't come seeking your forgiveness? Then what? Are you going to continue life holding on to your idea that they might come back and ask your forgiveness? Are you going to continue to hold that grudge? Will you drop the situation? How will you respond? Since I've matured in my relationship with Christ, I don't wait for others to come to me, even if they've done something wrong. Oftentimes I find myself genuinely forgiving an individual, forgetting (not bringing it up or bashing it in their ear as a constant reminder), giving it to God, and moving to my next assigned task. I wasn't this way all my life, but developing an intimacy with God surely helped.

What about the world we live in and the society that surrounds us? I mean, there are people who might come and ask your forgiveness, but you also have those who will not. When you are unforgiving the only person you hurt is you, because you continue to hold on to it. I read in a book that you have to forgive and love the individual by faith. And that's the truth!

Forgiveness does many things for a person. Well at least for me it does. Besides the fact that it breaks any opportunity for a satanic influence to keep a stronghold on you, I think of forgiveness like an antidote for revenge. You can't carry out God's plan if your heart can't forgive. Forgiveness erases those dark blemishes that might often try and stay lingering on your heart. To forgive means now you've kept your spirit from being damaged because of your decision.

What forgiveness does is strengthens our weaknesses and results in freedom, something that God has given to us over 2,000 years ago. Who knew forgiving could be so essential to our lives and important to continue our walk in Christ? I did—well, I learned.

Can I be vulnerable and transparent with you? I'm actually a very private person, but this is a great opportunity to share my imperfection with you. Growing up I had anger issues and the best way for me to release my anger, I felt, that made me feel better was if I was able to hurt someone, sometimes myself, or destroy something. At a young age I dealt with suicidal thoughts and attempts no one knew of. I withheld so much anger and didn't really understand why. I never really reached the root of my anger, but all I know now is that I've been delivered from it.

There were times that if my parents made me angry I would go in my room and punch walls. If I got angry at myself, I wanted to kill myself. There were a few times I attempted to puncture and cut on myself. There was even an incident when I punched my brother to the point he nearly lost control of his breath. I also wrote threatening letters to my sister plotting how I was going to kill her. There is more, but I'll save it all for later (maybe in another book). Where did it all derive from? I have no clue. I promise you I didn't share that for nothing. I want to specifically pinpoint my sister. Like other siblings, we have our good days and our bad days. Growing up, there were a bunch of things I know I did to her that she'll never forget, but there were also things she has done that I never forgave.

One day she went into my room without my permission and took some items. How did I find out? Thanks to Instagram, I can find out just about everything. Plus, I went home, before leaving to go to the store, to check to see if my items were there. They weren't. She knew that all she had to do was simply ask, but she couldn't even do that. Even if she did ask, if I didn't respond the way she wanted me to, she would still take them. Every time she and I disagreed, my anger toward her grew stronger and I never truly forgave her for those situations—I would just hold everything in and keep everything she'd done stored in a section of my brain. Whelp, this particular day when she went and got something from my room was the last straw. Everything and anything she had done up to that point was ready to be released. I felt like I was in one of those cartoons where they say, "Release the dragon" because that night I actually felt like one. I told God that I couldn't take it anymore. I yelled out of anger. Out of my mouth I even said, "I just want to kill her!"

So on my drive returning home from the store, not knowing she would be home already, I began plotting how I was going to hurt her. Then, the Holy Spirit began to calm me, but I wasn't trying to hear Him. I walked in the house, went straight to the kitchen to grab a knife, and walked into her room after noticing her light was on. I swung her white room door open with anger piercing my heart and aggressively stepped close to her face with the knife behind my back in the grip of my hands. Before acting in retaliation, I asked her, "Why did you take my things?" That was my grace, although I asked in a rude manner.

She responded with a disrespectful response that wasn't close to my satisfaction. I couldn't really move my hands quick enough because my brother came and removed the knife from my hand. So I choked her using both hands long enough to feed into exactly what Satan wanted. I stormed out of her room and went into my room to cry my anger away. Then, because I knew I was wrong and had sinned, I began to repent and apologize wholeheartedly to God. I told Him I knew I shouldn't have done that before I even arrived home to do it. I was convicted. I was torn because I gave the enemy something to feed and fuel from. Remember this: the enemy can only feed from whatever you're willing for him to have control over.

I called myself trying to apologize to her so she would return what belonged to me. It didn't work. Although I wanted to feel like I apologized, God and I both knew that the apology I gave wasn't from my heart.

A few days passed and no words were spoken between us. I knew she was highly upset with me, but at the same time it didn't bother me to know how she felt. Sunday came and my dad (Pastor Eric Jones, Sr. of The Messiah Empowering Word Church) spoke on forgiveness and obedience. His message couldn't have been more timely and precise. The message simply confirmed the very thing the Holy Spirit told me from God, which I already knew I was supposed to do. So after church I decided to be obedient to God. Although I didn't want to ask for her forgiveness, God wanted me to. I pulled my sister into a room and genuinely stated, "Look, I know what I did was wrong and out of anger. I know that I haven't authentically apologized, but I want to do that now." I continued with, "I genuinely apologize for choking you and it wasn't very Godly of me." I asked her, "Will you forgive me?"

Guess what? She didn't forgive me…I'm joking, she did forgive me. We exchanged hugs and to my surprise she immediately opened up to me and started talking to me. I was so pleased and overjoyed, first, because I obeyed God. But I was also overjoyed because I felt a release that allowed me to continue my walk with Christ. The enemy no longer had control over me.

Fuel to the Fire

Satan feeds off of negative energy and adds fuel to the fire. He likes to create a stir that will get and keep you disorderly. And I like to use my siblings as an example because they are the ones who used to upset me most; I made it my job to come back for them ten times stronger. But maybe that's just a universal sibling thing. We would always add fuel and heighten the fire. It only takes a little negativity to ignite a full fire. Remember that.

My siblings and I would always bicker over small things escalating those to big things and over big things creating bigger fires, just like normal siblings do, right? Well, if I were caught and got in trouble by my parents, my facial expression would change into that confused Scooby-doo look and the first thing from my mouth would be, "Huh, but she started it," or "she did it to me first." Between my sister and me, the argument would transfer back and forth and the revenge never stopped. We were those kids that lived by the saying, "That's payback from what you did last Sunday." I honestly believe we could have published a book called, "The Revengers" and it would've probably been a national best seller. I shared that because, if we pay attention, we do it ourselves and if we allow it, revenge can become uncontrollable. Revenge shouldn't be a "natural" consequence, but sometimes we allow our flesh to take over our minds and show through our actions.

My Bible relates revenge to a boomerang. But I'm going to call it the Boomerang Effect. Why? Because a boomerang never ceases and the effect of it comes with a cost. Revenge affects you and causes you to be blinded from love with retaliation and keeps an unhealthy cycle flowing in your life. Revenge only continues to ignite a raging fire that will eventually expand and spiral out of control. Revenge is not of God or obedient to His will—it comes with a cost. Break the cycle and replace revenge with love.

A boomerang, explained by Webster's Dictionary, "Is a curved flat piece of wood that is thrown and returned to the thrower. It cannot be thrown without a cost to the thrower."

To completely eradicate the Boomerang Effect you must forgive. I'm pretty sure you already knew what I was going to say.

Forgiveness is Freedom

To become free, barriers must be broken. Strongholds must be demolished. Priscilla Shirer is one of my spiritual leaders; I just enjoy reading her books and listening to her speak. I completed her book, *"Discerning the Voice of God"*, which is totally awesome by the way. She defined strongholds as "spiritual barricades that keep the voice of God from reaching our spiritual ear."

It makes me think of a brick wall and how every brick is a representation of a stronghold that shields you from seeing God and hearing Him. And sometimes it might very well feel as if every time you try taking a step closer to God you repeatedly run into the same brick or into multiple bricks in the wall. In this case the stronghold is unforgiveness, but isn't limited to result in such matters as low self-esteem, fear, doubt, pride, ungodly thoughts, sexual immorality and the list could go on. If you continue to make the cycle, you'll never get anywhere. Don't allow those strongholds to lay so heavily on you that you can't move forward in Jesus.

Strongholds are like steel chains that Satan uses as a "leash" to keep you locked. Satan comes to *kill, steal, and destroy* (John 10:10). And he seeks whom he may devour (1 Peter 5:8). I want to feed from the word "whom" in (1 Peter 5:8) because Satan can only attack you if you allow him to. The word "whom" can be an indicator that a person has to give permission for something to happen. It is his duty to make you feel as if those chains are truly weighing you down. Not being free to live in divine freedom that God has given to you.

We are in spiritual warfare. And although the battle is already won if you're on #teamJesus, the enemy will attack until the battle is completely over. Scripture tells us, *"For though we walk in the flesh, we do not war after the flesh."* (2 Corinthians 10:3). God has given us the essential armor to wear and use when the enemy tries to strike. It makes the enemy upset when it's difficult for him to have access to you. That's why your spiritual armor (The Word of God) must be on and you must be prepared at all times.

Ephesians even confirms to us that we can do exceedingly, abundantly, above all that we're able to ask or think according to the power that works within us (Ephesians 3:20). So the power is already within you, but to use that power to defeat the strongholds of the enemy requires being intimate with Jesus, praying, having faith, love, the Holy Spirit and knowing the Word of God. The Godly weapons gladly given to us are the only weapons that can break barriers. The enemy can be defeated and those bricks that you continue to walk into can be removed. I believe it starts with your mind, your thinking. If Satan can grab ahold of your mind, he will make you do anything to contaminate it. If you give Satan a centimeter, I guarantee he will do his best to take a mile.

Get this: once you have made up your mind not to allow the enemy in, you will have a mind-shift that will keep you moving forward in God. Your mind-shift will cause you to elevate in Christ. The enemy will no longer be able to control you. Once your thinking elevates for His good, His purpose, and what is pleasing to Him—it will cause a disconnection between the enemy and yourself. Don't become slaves to the enemy's purpose: strongholds.

Leviticus 26:13 reads *"I am the Lord your God, which brought you forth out of the land of Egypt, that ye shall not be their bondmen; and I have broken the bands of your yoke, and made you go upright."* God has allowed us to live a life of freedom in Him. You are no longer a slave held captive to your sins, your burdens, and your strongholds. Your mind is no longer subject to what the enemy has you thinking and no longer will you be buried in shame. It is only a trick of Satan to keep you in denial, misery and chained away from freedom. Don't be a prisoner to it.

In your mind, you have to know that God has forgiven you and wiped your slate clean. That your past doesn't dictate your future plans and the purpose God has created for you before coming out your mother's womb (Jeremiah 1:5). Because God has forgiven you, you are free! The way to continue living in that freedom is to follow after Jesus' footsteps in forgiving others and loving others as He loves you.

Don't Retaliate, Forgive

There are people I know who mistake the idea of forgiveness, or should I say, asking for forgiveness from others as a sign of weakness. In reality it isn't. They believe that if they don't do tit-for-tat then it is also a sign of weakness.

The book of 1 Kings in the first chapter is a story about Solomon becoming king. There was a huge uproar about who would succeed their aging King David when he passed: Solomon or Adonijah? Adonijah posed as the king, but Solomon was actually appointed by David to succeed him. Adonijah (David's fourth son) was doing things he wasn't supposed to do and Solomon received word of it. Of course when Adonijah had to face Solomon, he asked King Solomon to spare his life (v. 51). King Solomon, a wise man, dismissed the altercation and sent his brother on.

At that moment, realize that although Solomon had the power to kill Adonijah, he forgave. In this case, Solomon was the stronger person because he did not retaliate. He didn't have to prove his power and he certainly wasn't a weak man. If you think about it, forgiving or seeking forgiveness shows and takes more strength than having the last say. You should read the rest and find out what happens next!

Remember this: retaliation doesn't make you the "bigger" person in any way and neither does it make you the strongest. It means that you lack self-control in forgiveness.

So, I Forgave, Now What?

Most times, after we've forgiven a person, what to do next is probably never carefully thought through. We just tend to go about our days knowing what happened, but not necessarily putting away what has happened for good. I bet you're sitting there wondering what the next step to this forgiving method is. It's quite simple! I have three methods to this madness: permitting yourself to forgive, forget, and love, living in freedom, and remaining prayerful.

1. **Permit yourself to forgive, forget, and love.**

   I know, I know. Forget? How can I forget what someone has done to me? We're human, we won't literally forget. We cannot selectively "erase" life events from our minds. What I mean by 'forget,' is to simply not bring it up. Don't refer back to past events. We should choose to 'forgive and forget' for the sake of Christ and move on with our lives. Remember, God sees all and knows all, but yet and still He forgives and forgets and no longer counts our sins against us.

1 John 4:11 tells us, *"Beloved, if God so loved us, we also ought to love one another."* We have to love. Love yourself and God, while allowing God to love on you and show love through you.

2. **Move forward and live in freedom.**

What I love about God is that He desires for us to live a stress-free, liberated life. The freedom I'm speaking of is a divine freedom that can only be lived through Christ. The fact is that we are prisoners of sin in this world. The only way to be free is in Jesus. Second Corinthians 3:17 tells us, *"Now the Lord is that Spirit: and where the Spirit of the Lord is, there is liberty."*

To attain that liberty and live in it, we must first move forward. We can't dwell on the incidents that have happened and we certainly can't just wallow in a pity party. God wants to shift us out of our mess, but we have to want to do it ourselves as well.

3.   **Remain Prayerful**

First Thessalonians tells us to *"Pray without ceasing."* Therefore the most important thing to do is to remain prayerful at all times. After you forgive, continue to keep a prayerful heart and continue to remain prayerful in all that you do and are faced with all the while walking in love. Constantly being prayerful and walking in love can sometimes be a difficult thing to do.

Sometimes I ask Jesus, "Man, how do you do it?" Just like that. He reminds me that I can walk in love because He lives within me and because He left specific instructions on how to walk in love daily. He also reminds me that praying doesn't always mean you have to be on your knees, but throughout my day I can pray—at work, at the store, in the car, and so on. Pray without ceasing.

All of these keys are essential to restoration. They are essential to being able to move forward, not just for yourself, but in Christ. We are to be obedient to the commandments of God. I agree that sometimes being a

Christian is a struggle. But because I love God and because I want to make my way into heaven to see Him, I'm going to obey and do what is pleasing unto Him.

People will continue to hurt us as well as leave scars. Just as people hurt us, it's worth being cognizant that we probably have indented scars on someone us. But it's all about perspective, the way we look at things. We have a choice: We can either find a positive or remain angry at what has been done to us. We can consciously decide to make an effort to keep our minds focused on our loving Father, God, and the growing relationship we are steadily building with Him—knowing, trusting, and believing His Word. If you don't capture anything else from this chapter, remember this: God has a plan for our lives. He's looking at our hearts and our attitudes. And I might add, forgiveness is not contingent on the actions of others, but simply on our attitudes.

With Love & Sincerity,

-Veronica D. Jones

About Veronica Jones

Veronica Jones is a 23-year-old Dallas native who enjoys family, books, mentoring, and empowering women. As the founder of She's Empowered to Create (shesetc.org), she finds herself passionate about encouraging and serving women/young ladies through sharing her personal experiences. Not only is she passionate about conquering fears and situations, but is intentionally passionate about helping women conquer their fears and move forward in Christ.

Veronica is a philanthropist, speaker, mentor, and aspiring author. She finds peace in being able to voluntarily serve others. It is through her experiences that she has become a relevant voice along with a burst of passion, service, kindness, tenacity, laughter, and boldness all combined toward a sweet fragrance of helping others. She's a former TCU track athlete, who is definitely on the track that leads to helping you push out more, whether you're wanting to discover "more" or add "more" to your life.

Contact Information

Facebook: Veronica Jones

Instagram: @veronicadjones_

Email: vjones@shesetc.org

Web: veronicadjones.com

THEREFORE; *Forgive. Love. and. Rest*

BETTY KOSSICK

"And we know that all things work together for good to those who love God, to those who are the called according to His purpose."

Romans 8:28

Because of Prayer

Are you praying for God to use you in ministry? Are you filled with desire to be His servant, but don't know what exactly to do? Are you willing to get out of your comfort zone to do it? If you answer, "Yes," to all three of these questions, you're either on your way to ministry or already there.

Elizabeth remembers when she first started praying for God to give her a ministry, one with a unique purpose to bring honor and glory to His name. In her late 30s, married with nearly grown children, her prayers continued something like this, day after day, "Lord, I pray every day to be a blessing. But I feel that I can do more now that my children are almost adults. I'm asking for a special ministry to do for You." That prayer continued for three years.

Elizabeth also claimed Psalm 119:65-66, "Do good to your servant according to Your word, O, Lord. Teach me your knowledge and good judgment for I believe in Your commands."

A part of her desire to serve the Lord more fully came from learning the meaning of her name, Elizabeth:

Consecrated to God. Her first five years were not founded with a Christian yardstick, her parent didn't give her that name to live up to; she was simply named after a grandmother she never knew. Yet learning her name's meaning in adulthood helped prepare her with a want to do something to make a difference, such as helping people beat the nicotine habit. Though not a smoker herself, she had seen so many people suffer ill health and die from the habit; and God laid it upon her heart to help others quit. The pastor of her church, her husband and other church members held the same desire.

Thus, in the late 1960s, her pastor launched free smoking cessation classes, designed by physicians for smokers who wanted to escape the life-ebbing habit. The classes proved successful. And out of those early classes a relationship developed with Dr. John Morely, the Director of the Health Department in Akron, Ohio, to present stop-smoking classes at the Health Department. Thus, the efforts of those who assisted the pastor were coupled with the sanction of the city's health leader. Many people escaped the bondage of nicotine addiction through those meetings.

Elizabeth, though unschooled in public relations, nonetheless served in that capacity for the classes, contacting media sources and setting the information-stage previous to each series of meetings. Part of her task was to serve as a receptionist when the participants arrived. Doubt nagged her, *Will these people, who are trying to quit, trust someone who's never been addicted?*

No problem. Not only did those who attended respond, but some lifetime friendships resulted. Of those hundreds who were helped, Evey is one. She recently turned 90 years old. As she celebrated her nonagenarian birthday, she realized this birthday would not have happened if she'd continued on her path of self-destruction through smoking. Elizabeth found that friendships that are formed with strangers are bonuses that come with the ministry of service to others.

Because of the success of the smoking-cessation classes, Elizabeth was asked to serve her church in a public relations capacity. In the 1960s, her PR skills were this—typing: two fingers; college classes: none; PR experience: none; no training in how to write a press release, and no communication degrees. Apprehension dogged her. The smoking-cessation classes were her only education and experience.

However, press releases that she submitted to the Akron Beacon Journal caught the attention of Pete Geiger, the Religion Page editor. He told Elizabeth, "You should be getting paid for what you're doing."

She thought he was just being nice. She told him that she was a novice.

He seemed startled and replied, "You're doing everything right." Then he asked her, "What else do you do for ministry?" After sharing with him, he asked her to write an article for the newspaper's religion page about how to share Christ.

The light bulb went on! Elizabeth realized that her three years of prayer for a special ministry was happening! At age 40!

Subsequently, letters to the owner/editor of a weekly newspaper, *The Signal*, resulted in her being invited to meet the editor. By this time, her byline also was appearing regularly in the religious and poetry press. The editor, Allen Etling, wanted to talk to her about working as a freelancer for his newspaper. The meeting between Elizabeth and the editor was set for three days away. Talk about feeling out of her comfort zone: She felt petrified. She asked herself, *why did I agree to meet up with him?* She tossed and turned and prayed and prayed each night. The meeting occurred. She got the job.

Then, just as her ministry expanded, she and her husband moved away from the Akron area for his work. *Is my work as a writer short-lived, already done?* she questioned herself.

Yet the move away to another Ohio town, Kettering, led to freelance work with a large metropolitan newspaper: *Dayton Daily News*. However, three years later her husband's work as a trouble-shooter electrician took them to California. Then, they were off to Kansas, and then back to Ohio. All these moves were working with Seventh-day Adventist hospitals.

After her husband retired, God still led them to other places to serve Him: Michigan, Florida, Georgia, and back again to Florida. Every place they moved, God reserved a writing ministry for Elizabeth to touch lives and honor Him. Always, a ministry waited. Their first time in Florida offered an abundance of outreach, when she hopped on board with

Zephyrhills News. Thus, each move enlarged her sphere of service. And as lay members, she and her husband, Johnny continued as a team to serve their church and communities with a variety of assistance programs, such as United Way and Love in the Name of Christ.

Reaching back to freelancing for the first newspaper, she realizes daily that she was called by God to be a journalist. Along the way, she managed to attend college, interview world-famous people, and is the recipient of various awards for her writing and recognition for her community involvement. No longer relegated to the corner of her kitchen to write, certificates and plaques line the walls of her office. She gives thanks daily to God's appointment for service and the results of prayer.

There is a 10-word quote in the book *Prophets and Kings*, pg. 486, that Elizabeth says has been a guide for her, "God gives opportunities; success depends on the use made of them."

Elizabeth discovered early on that it isn't her writing alone that serves both the secular and religious press; it's being honest, dependable, and others-motivated. Versatility in writing is highly valued by editors as well. A Christian writer is under scrutiny for his or her ethics more so than one who makes no claim that Jesus is their friend. She didn't want to in any way vilify His name. The mettle of her personal Christianity met many tests, such as only accepting assignments that were worthy stories, meeting deadlines, and all the ethical requirements editors want, need, and demand. In the mix there were assignments that she turned down. By so doing, the editors instead of not retaining her in their writers' pool, continue providing assignments. Her witness was and is valued. And often the opportunity arose to pray with the editors.

Yet, it isn't always writing that provides her ministry. The opportunities came by interacting with people, praying with her interviewees (in one town she received the moniker "the praying reporter"), and seeing people blessed. To recall sitting at the longest boardroom table imaginable and praying in that huge room with the top executive—and see his tears plop on the highly polished table top as she prayed with him, humbled her.

To pray with four-star general Norman Schwarzkopf did likewise, and to interview Col. Jim Irwin, astronaut, to ask him what he'd have asked God when he went to the moon and to hear his humble answer, "Do I have Your permission to be here?" Then to sit in Alex Haley's private office in Los Angeles, to quiz the Noble prize-winning author of *Roots*, added to her joy as she questioned him about his *spiritual* roots. She knew she was in the role she'd prayed for—to serve God in a special way.

Elizabeth also finds in her work many people who never before enjoyed the privilege of prayer with anyone. Delightful friendships result. All the prayers with whomever affirm to her that her own prayers to serve and honor God were answered. To her, the most amazing aspect of it all is this: if she hadn't prayed that prayer for ministry, none of these experiences would be hers. When people ask her where she received her education and training, she tells them confidently, "The University of the Holy Spirit."

There is another aspect of ministry that she's enjoyed immensely—and that is passing on the torch, as she teaches others to write. That privilege first started in Cadillac, Michigan, when she worked as a freelancer for *Cadillac News* in the mid to late '90s. She developed two classes of her own, "Beyond Being a Wanna-Be," a how-to freelance writers' class, as well as a class for upper-elementary students, "The Fun of Writing." Both classes have turned out numerous published writers. When her students learn to say with confidence, "I am a writer!" Elizabeth is overjoyed. To see their bylines is far more thrilling to her than to see her own.

"Prayer is the key to service in whatever your ministry," she says. Trusting in Him to send his Holy Spirit to guide is foremost, she continually discovers. Most of all, through her journey as a writer she came to the understanding of the value in trusting God completely—and not to do anything without prayer. She finds great delight in the admonition of Proverbs 3:5-6, "Trust in the Lord with all your heart, and lean not on your own understanding; in all your ways acknowledge Him, And He shall direct your paths."

Elizabeth is an ordinary woman to whom God allowed some extra-ordinary experiences. She says that she relates to the unlearned fishermen whom Jesus beckoned to follow Him. Jesus is The Teacher for those who say "Yes," to His call. She didn't hanker to be a writer; she didn't plan it. In fact, if you'd have told her that at age 40 she'd become a writer, she'll tell you that she'd probably have done a laughing-Sarah act. You know, like when Sarah got the news in her elderly age that she'd give birth to a baby.

The development of Elizabeth's story didn't occur as happenstance. God planned it all—because of prayer. Her story fits the Relationships God-Style motto: **H**ealing (her work is her healing balm for physical pain and emotional pain that comes with life's sorrows—it is her meds and she's found that it also heals others), her writing provides **E**ncouragement for readers, her words are filled with **L**ove, they provide **P**eace for the worried and weary, and her writing grants her ongoing answer to her prayer: a **P**urpose in serving God.

To this assignment she repeats these words from 1 Timothy 1:12, "I thank Christ Jesus our Lord, who has given me strength, that He considered me faithful, appointing me to His service." This can be your thank you to Jesus every day as you venture into a faithful, purposeful ministry to elevate His name.

This is not a fiction story, this is a true story. I know because, you see, I am Elizabeth.

About Betty Kossick

Betty Kossick holds a 44-year writing career as a freelance journalist, with her feature stories, news writing, and columns appearing in California, Florida, Georgia, Kansas, Michigan and Ohio newspapers. Her work also appears in religious and secular magazines on a regular basis. She is also the author of a writer's manual: *Basic Writing Skills*, published by *Advent Source*. She interviewed the subjects for Jane Boucher's book *Escaping Domestic Abuse*. In addition, Betty's works both in prose and poetry appear in anthologies, devotional books, and short story compilations for a total of 66 books, with others slated for publication in 2015 and 2016. Her volunteer writing consists mostly of press releases and feature articles.

A late bloomer, who started writing at age 40, an ongoing career in journalism continues to evolve with the interview as her forte. Her early traumatic childhood, her emerging walk with God, and an unexpected career as a writer, all supply the fodder for her autobiographical book *Beyond the Locked Door* (2006), available through Internet books sites such as Amazon.com. She also solo authored a book of poetry, *Heart Ballads,* in 2009.

Recognition for excellence in journalism and as a role model have brought her awards such as a Michigan Press Award, Woman of Worth, Celebrate Women!, Carroll Award, Listen America Eagle Award, and others. However, when she sees those to whom she's taught writing skills succeed with published work, she considers those her best awards.

THEREFORE; *Forgive, Love, and Rest*

PATRICIA MANNING

"I can do all things through Christ which strengtheneth me."

Philippians 4:13

I Know Something about God's Grace

I am the youngest of four children—two boys and two girls. My mother was a single parent until she wed when I was about nine years old. I remember attending Our Mother of Mercy Church as a very young child and was given a New Testament Bible that I would read religiously. Our Mother of Mercy was a Catholic church. I wouldn't be introduced to Baptist churches until much later in my life.

I was a tomboy growing up. I hung with the fellas and played kickball, football, basketball, baseball, climbed trees, hopped trains, built go carts, shot bb guns, etc., etc. I acquired a high tolerance to pain because when you hung with the boys, you couldn't cry. You had to take a lickin' and keep on tickin'. If you cried, you had to go home and that would put an end to your run with the guys.

My childhood was pretty normal. Later in my teen years (my senior year in high school, to be exact), I met and fell head over heels in love with a young man who would become the father of my oldest child. I was of the belief that I would not ever feel about anyone the way I felt about him. He was my first love (not my first boyfriend) and our relationship was rocky at best. He attended our rival high school (we only had two in the district) and was the quarterback of the football team no less. He also was dating a girl who attended my high school as well as two that attended his. I had come to the realization that he would not be mine alone, so I opted to take something away from the relationship. When I found out I was pregnant, I suddenly realized what effect it might have on my mother. I was 22 years old and working for Exxon and living at home. To my surprise and relief, my mother was ecstatic. I guess it was about having her first grandchild.

I chose to raise my son, Eric, alone. I was diagnosed as a Type 1 diabetic at the age of 24, two years after the birth of my son. I was always on the "skinny" side, and the most weight I ever gained was when I was pregnant. I immediately lost the weight I had gained, but a little too much. I continued to "lose weight" for the next two years after I had given birth and it took my sister to notice first. She saw me with no shirt on and commented, "You look like you are anorexic.

My mother dismissed it and I didn't realize it until I went shopping one day and bought some pants. I tried them on before I paid for them, but did not wear them until about 3 days later and they were too big. I also had a big appetite and an unquenchable thirst (which did not mean anything to me at the time). I would mention my lack of weight gain after the birth of my son and my doctor would dismiss it saying, some women would kill to be my size. After I continued to lose weight and after the comment made by my sister, I became concerned and I wrote a letter to my OBGYN and told him what was going on. He put me in the hospital for nine days and ran all kinds of tests and discovered my diabetes. He asked me if any members of my family were diabetic and I stated no, because I did not know of any.

While I was hospitalized my oldest brother visited me and when I told him I was a diabetic, he told me that my grandparents were both diabetic on my father's side. This was my first time hearing my godfather referenced as my father. Up until then, I had called this man my godfather because he had been in my life and I was never told anything different. I also learned that he was the biological father to my youngest brother. My father never married and my brother and I were his only two children, but that is another story for another time. So I have spent the past 32 years injecting myself with insulin as many as four times a day every day. I often prayed for God to remove this thorn in my flesh, but I was reminded of His word that says, "My grace is sufficient for thee."

Along with my being a Type 1 diabetic, I have had many other medical issues: hysterectomy for a dropping uterus (being diabetic caused the lining of my uterus not to repair itself after giving birth), endometrioses (surgery), internal rectal hemorrhoids (surgery), oral surgery for gum disease, and surgery on my right hand for my index finger getting stuck in the down position (a form of carpal tunnel). Though I wasn't sick as a child, I have had to become used to a few "bumps in the road" concerning my health as an adult.

I accepted Christ as my Lord and Savior shortly after the death of my mother on August 8, 1987. She was 58 years old and a lifetime smoker. She died of a heart attack, as did my grandmother who was also a smoker. I was new in the faith and read the Word constantly and was very active in ministry. It was then that I started praying for a husband. I knew, from a brief marriage earlier, that I needed to pray this time. My criteria for a man was that he accept my son and treat him like his own and preferably have a child or children of his own as siblings for my son.

Well, I believe Satan also heard my prayer and he sent a decoy. I met my 2nd husband through a fellow church member and co-worker (she also was working for Exxon, but in a different area), who had no idea what I had prayed for. So being a babe in Christ, I believed God had answered my prayer. He was divorced and had custody of his two children, a boy and a girl. He would come to church and he would also read the Bible. Satan knows the Word as well. I didn't realize until much later in my growth that I should have prayed for a *saved* husband who loves the Lord and serves Him. He talked the talk, but didn't walk the walk. He said and did all of the right things before we married. Based on my experience, I believe his true identity didn't emerge until much later.

It wasn't all bad, I must admit. He had some good qualities and provided for our every need. We would take two vacations a year, one for the kids and one for us. We moved into his home, which was several miles outside of Houston and while Eric lived with my husband, John and his children full time, I would stay in Houston during the week and come home on the weekends, which was why I didn't see his true nature right away. I moved to Freeport full time after our son, Charles was born, and spent the next three years commuting to Houston for work, some 60 miles one way and would bring Charles along to attend day care. It was then that I started seeing John's dark side, because he couldn't keep it hidden 24/7. He was verbally and physically abusive to the children when disciplining them and verbally abusive to me. Eric was spared his wrath because he was a good child. Eric did what he was told and he did well in school. And when he witnessed the way that the others were disciplined, he avoided any wrongdoing at all cost.

I was not aware of the type of disciplining the children were enduring until I overheard them talking about it while eating dinner and my husband was not at home. They were actually joking about it, but I was horrified! I started intervening on their behalf, threatening to call law enforcement if he continued to use inappropriate discipline. It stopped, only for him to focus his verbal abuse toward me.

One night after the children had gone to bed, I was in the bedroom reading and he was in the living room watching television. I was getting ready to go to bed and went to the kitchen for a glass of water. On the dining room table was a loaded hand gun. He was an avid gun collector and kept them locked up in the gun cabinet; although, he carried one in the van and had another at the top of the bedroom closet. I was angry that the gun was out and accessible because Charles slept in the bedroom across from the dining room with his sister. He was only two years old and could have gotten up and picked up the gun and hurt himself.

I closed their bedroom door and at first I was going to confront him, because I felt that it was a threat against my life. I was not comfortable with guns and did not know how to handle one and felt that if I would have moved it or said something to him about it, things would have just gotten ugly. Instead, I went into the bedroom and began to pray, "Now I lay me down to sleep, I pray the Lord my soul to keep. If I should die before I wake, I pray the Lord my soul to take." I then went to sleep in perfect peace.

We separated a short time later and divorced after 10 years of marriage (7 years of separation). I knew that God had kept me through the death of my mother, a bad marriage and divorce, health issues, a layoff, foreclosure, the death of my father, bankruptcy and the death of my brother, and that

He proved as good as His Word, that He would never leave me nor forsake me. Little did I know that my faith would be put to the test yet again.

Psalm 121:1, 2, I will lift my eyes unto the hills, from whence cometh my help? My help cometh from the Lord, which made heaven and earth.

I was diagnosed with Stage II breast cancer in May 2009. It started as so many of my mammograms had started before. I would have the mammogram and then my doctor would call to request that I have an ultrasound because of something that appeared on the mammogram. And after the ultrasound, I would be told that the ultrasound was negative.

So when my doctor requested I have an ultrasound, I really didn't give it much thought. Well, this time my ultrasound revealed that I had two tumors and would need to have a biopsy. I felt a little anxious by this time, but still believed that all would be well. After all, my mother had tumors in her breast and they turned out to be benign.

I was attending a Family Team Meeting at one of my offices at work when my secretary called stating my doctor needed to get in touch with me and I needed to call him. He had called my office phone and got my voicemail and pressed 0 to reach the secretary. So I stepped out of my meeting and called. So many things went through my mind while I was dialing, but I decided I would keep a positive frame of mind.

He started by asking me where I was and would I be able to come to his office so he could give me my test results. I want to stop here and give some background about my doctor. He has been my doctor for 33 years and delivered both of my children. So when he requested that I come into the office to obtain my results, I asked him to just give them to me over the phone. He said they don't like to give test results over the phone.

That's when alarm bells went off in my head. I had received test results over the phone before, such as the other times when my ultrasound results were negative and even when the test results would come back from my pap smears and the result was that I had a yeast infection and they were calling my pharmacy with a prescription. And at that moment I realized that it was usually his nurse who would call and for the doctor himself to be calling made it even more alarming.

I told him that I had known him all of these years; I didn't know how long this meeting would last (It was already after 4:30), and I was giving him permission to just tell me over the phone! And it was then that I received the news that no woman wants to hear: one of the two tumors was malignant.

I asked him, "Okay, what is next?" And he said that he would refer me to an Oncologist, gave me the number and stated that it was caught early and urged me to call the Oncologist as soon as possible to begin my treatment.

I returned to the meeting feeling numb. I sent out a mass text message telling family and friends about the test results, not realizing the responses I would get. My phone immediately blew up with text messages and phone calls. I realized that that was not a smart thing to do. I informed my church family of my diagnosis and immediately received the "praying for you", "if you need anything…" and the altar prayer for me, and the beginning of my descent down the rabbit hole.

My treatment plan was six rounds of chemo treatments to shrink the tumors and then surgery to remove them. I was given a cocktail of drugs that was a total of about five different chemo drugs and I was informed that I would get sicker with each round of chemo. I was given the chemo via a port that was surgically implanted and the chemo given via IV into the port. My treatments were every three weeks that included an after-chemo shot that I was given the next day after the chemo treatment.

My hair began coming out by the second treatment and it wasn't until I could no longer taste my food and grew too sick to continue to work that depression set in and my crying out to the Lord became more intense.

My oldest son was living in his own apartment and my younger son was in and out of jail during the time of my treatments, so for the most part, I was home alone with my three dogs. The reason I described my experience of breast cancer as a descent down a rabbit hole is because of the feelings of loneliness, depression, darkness and despair. I stopped going to church because I was so sick and I was getting weaker by the day. I was still able to drive myself to my treatments until the very last one when I was driven by a friend and taken into treatment via a wheelchair.

"I can do all things through Christ who strengthens me" (Phil 4:13). This is the scripture that helped me through my sickness.

About the time of my third chemo treatment, I could no longer taste any food. A white coating had completely covered my tongue. My day was spent getting up in the morning and attempting to eat breakfast. I learned that I had to eat to live, not live to eat. I would go into my living room to watch TV and/or read. I spent a lot of time in the book of Psalms because it seemed to speak on what I was going through. I spent a lot of time and money buying food that I would try to eat, only to get sick and end up giving it to the dogs. I must say they ate well in the beginning. I would end my day going to bed and having sleepless nights due to being in pain and feeling sick.

I would pray for the Lord to allow me a good night's sleep, but as the treatments progressed restlessness and sleepless nights prevailed. "It is written: 'Man shall not live on bread alone, but on every word that comes from the mouth of God'" Luke 4:4. I was so hungry watching television commercials about people eating and enjoying food, it brought me to tears! It is about this time that I became angry with God.

I couldn't sleep, couldn't eat and my physical strength was failing me. I cried uncontrollably and would purposely watch sad movies to give myself a reason to cry. I was so sad and depressed. I questioned God, not so much as to why this was happening to me, but more so why He continued to allow me to wake up the next morning, only to suffer more pain and hunger.

If I had to say one positive thing about me it is that I have a good sense of humor. I like to think that I got it from both of my parents, because they loved to laugh and joke. My sense of humor was long gone. I tried to watch funny movies to try to make myself laugh and lighten up my mood, but it didn't work.

Like I said, I had stopped going to church or anywhere for that matter. I had convinced myself that I had to be very careful about being around people because my immune system was shot and I didn't want to risk getting a cold or the flu, because it was now winter time. I had very few visitors that I would let come to the house, mostly because of my dogs and most people are afraid of dogs, especially pit bulls of which I had one full-blooded male and a female pit bull mix. My other dog is a Chihuahua.

I would have offers to bring me food and I declined because I knew I couldn't eat it and sometimes just the smell would make me nauseous. I read the Word more and more, trying to find some comfort and peace. No man is an island, but isolation is just what Satan wanted. I was weak and vulnerable. I was in a dark place descending further into my rabbit hole.

By the time I completed by last chemo treatment in November 2009, I had shrunk from 160lbs to 95lbs (on a 5'6" frame) and my diet consisted of soup and Ensure. I barely could get out of the bed, so I would just lay there and groan. It was then that I could relate to the church songs that talk about moaning and groaning. I could relate to a lot of things that I took for granted. Since I was weak and worn, God had my undivided attention and brought back things to my remembrance.

He reminded me that I once was very active in ministry but became a "pew member" once my father passed away in 2002. How I would listen with indifference to testimonies because it was the same people Sunday after Sunday.

Whenever the musicians would play the "Holy Ghost" music, the same people would be the ones dancing and how annoyed I would get if they played too long. How I often stayed home from church functions, just because. Now I would give anything to be back in the service one more time, hear the choir play and Pastor preach. I longed for the fellowship one with another. He also made me realize that people need people. I am used to being independent and doing things for myself and He showed me that I could do nothing without Him and fellow Christians He was working through. I had people praying for me because I could no longer pray for myself. "The effectual and fervent prayers of a righteous man availeth much" (James 5:16).

I had my double mastectomy the first week in December 2009. Although I only had tumors in my right breast, I made the choice to have both breasts removed, because I wanted to lessen my chances of going through this again. My surgeon asked me if I was sure about having the double mastectomy because they wanted to be sure I was not making my decision based on emotions. I told him that I was sure, that I was not using them anyway.

He recommended that I wait before having reconstructive surgery. I had not decided if I was going to do that anyway. I was taken to the hospital by a good family friend and church member who stayed with me until I came out of surgery. My surgeon was also a Christian and I felt God's presence all around me. I had one of my church members to visit me in the hospital and brought me breast cancer items; a pink blanket, a pink bracelet with the breast cancer symbol, a pink pin of the breast cancer symbol, another bracelet with the breast cancer symbol carved into it and pink gummies candies enclosed in a pink zippered box with the breast cancer symbol, all of which I treasure and wear proudly to this day. I wasn't a big fan of the color pink, being a tomboy and all. Although my mother tried dressing me in pink, I rebelled because pink was a girly color and I needed to be tough to hang with the fellas. Now I have a deeper appreciation for the color pink. It symbolizes that I am a survivor.

I was discharged from the hospital on December 4, 2009. It had snowed all night the night before and still was snowing that morning. A friend had picked me up from the hospital and after retrieving my pain meds from the pharmacy, I went home to begin my recovery process. I was still weak, but the chemo had begun to wear off and my taste buds were slowly coming back. When I arrived home I made me some toast, took my medication and was going to lie down.

My son Charles was home and on the phone and outside taking pictures of the snow. Before I retreated into my bedroom, he came inside the house with a friend of his carrying a big box with Guitar Hero on it. I stopped them and questioned them about the item. Suffice it to say that Charles had been hanging with some unsavory characters who I believed to have sticky fingers. Charles assured me that this was "his" that he brought it over from his house, an alleged Christmas present belonging to his friend who lived in the neighborhood, and he wanted Charles to "keep" it for him. It didn't pass the smell test but I was medicated and just wanted to go and lay down. I told them both that he could "keep" it for him today, but tomorrow I wanted it out of my house.

I then went into my bedroom to lay down and got on a call from a co-worker who was checking on me. I may have been talking to her for about 10 minutes when I heard someone calling out to me, "Ms. Manning, Ms. Manning." Because my door was closed I didn't recognize who it was.

I got off of the phone and opened my door to two police officers in my hallway: one white male officer and one black female officer. They asked to speak to me and I headed toward my living room. Well, the female officer looked behind her and saw that I was coming with my dogs following me and she retrieved her gun and I started yelling for her not to shoot my dogs! She apparently had a fear of dogs and they were only puppies then and were not barking or growling. The male officer wasn't having any problems but I took the dogs back into my bedroom and closed the door. When I made it into my living room, there were five more officers gathered there and some were questioning Charles.

Apparently Charles's "friend" had actually broke into his parents' house and was stealing Christmas presents, one of which he brought to my house and others he had stashed at another friend's house. His parents had come home and caught him in the act and he ran off. The police were called and he was arrested at a store in the neighborhood. He told them where the items were and implicated both Charles and Caleb (the other friend) as his accomplices.

I informed the police that Charles was home alone when I got home from the hospital and his friend came to my house carrying the item and told me that it was his. Charles claimed to have not known that it had been stolen. Charles got the item from out of the garage and the officers stated that they needed him to come to the station to give his statement. I again informed the officers that I had just had major surgery and could not bring him and they stated that they would take him and bring him back.

Again, this did not pass the smell test, but I told them okay and if anything, hopefully Charles would learn a lesson from this (well, he didn't, but that's a story for another time). They left, I laid down and when I awoke some five hours later and Charles had not come home, I knew what time it was. He later called and confirmed that he and Caleb were arrested for receiving stolen property, but I don't recall the details. All I know is that I had been praying for Charles and for peace in my house and I felt like my prayers were not being heard. God knew that I would need time to heal, so He removed Charles long enough for that to happen.

I had my drainage tubes removed after about a week and was able to take my first shower. I gathered my tee shirt, bra and panties and headed into the bathroom. And then it hit me and I exploded in laughter. There is was, a sound that I had not heard in a very long time. It was the sound of my own laughter from deep down in my soul.

What was I laughing at you ask? Why it was the fact that out of habit I grabbed my bra. I continued to laugh at myself and even sent text messages to my friends telling them what I had done! They began to laugh at me and with me. Then I proceeded to take my shower and it happened again. I went to grab at my breast to lift them up to clean and I was grabbing at air! I laughed so hard I cried. Not from a sense of loss, but from the fact that God had brought me through. I was grateful. My sense of humor had returned. The darkness went away. I ascended from my rabbit hole. There was light at the end of the tunnel!

When I went for my follow up with the Oncologist, I thought he was going to release me to go back to work. Much to my dismay, he informed me that I still had to have surgery on my lymph nodes. Because I had Stage II breast cancer, it meant that the cancer had spread to my lymph nodes and I would have to have surgery to remove them.

So I made an appointment with my surgeon and had the lymph nodes removed in February 2010. He told me that he removed 37 lymph nodes and only one of them had cancer but I would not need to have any more chemo or radiation because it was removed. Praise God! I had my life back!

My appetite slowly returned and I was gaining weight and strength! I went back to work and more importantly, back to church! I had an attitude of gratitude! I thanked my Pastor and my church family for their prayers and support. I got off of the pew and started back to serving in ministry. It was no one but God and God alone who brought me through.

There was nothing like being hungry and not being able to eat that increased my compassion for those who are less fortunate and have to go without. I am an active financial supporter of our food bank and am very attentive to the prayer requests and needs of others. I am a firm believer in intercessory prayer.

I attended my first Breast Cancer Walk with the Sister's Network, but while I didn't have the energy to actually walk the three miles in April 2010, I wanted to show my support to other survivors as well as members of my church as they showed their support for me and others like me. Life was good again…but God was not through with me yet!

Every year my church recognizes breast cancer awareness month with the wearing of Pink and the breast cancer ribbons. The first year of my survival, they asked me to read a poem for the occasion. Now, I am not one for public speaking. In fact I get really nervous when I have to speak in front of people. I have to do it a lot with my job of supervising a staff of eight, testifying in court, conducting unit meetings, etc., but it still is not easy for me.

The next year they asked another survivor to speak and the following couple of years they just recognized the breast cancer survivors as well as the survivors of any cancer and the relatives of those who lost their lives due to cancer.

In September of 2013, I was approached by a member of the Women's Ministry counsel and asked to again speak the following month for breast cancer awareness. That feeling of dread washed over me about speaking in front of the congregation, so I told her that I would get back with her. September 17, 2013, about a little after midnight, I was feeling restless and couldn't fall asleep. I had a lot on my mind concerning work. We have what is called pending cases (cases that are over 60 days) and the pressure is on to get these cases closed. My mind was going a million miles a minute.

I finally got up and turned on the light. I was feeling kind of funny, so I checked my blood sugar to see if it was low. It was 84, so I decided I would and fix myself a bowl of cereal to bring my levels up.

At the same time, I was talking to one of my dogs (Big Boy) and the sound of my voice was disturbing. I was talking slow and slurring my words. Big Boy was tilting his head and looking at me funny. I tried eating the cereal and couldn't not chew. I had to manually move my jaw and the milk was running out of the corner of my mouth. I managed to finish eating and went back to bed, but couldn't sleep, still feeling out of sorts.

Charles was serving a five year prison sentence for aggravated robbery, so Eric had moved back home. I decided to wake him up to tell him what was going on with me. He discerned that I was having a stroke and called 911.

By the time the ambulance arrived, my speech had returned to normal. They checked my vital signs and did an EKG and all was normal. They suggested that I contact my primary care physician later on that morning and to call them back again if I continued to have difficulties. Eric stayed up for a little while longer and I again attempted to go back to bed.

After about 30 minutes and still feeling discombobulated Eric called the EMTs back and they took me to the emergency room. They immediately performed an MRI and admitted me into the hospital.

Several hours later, the emergency room doctor informed me that I had indeed had a mini-stroke which I still found hard to believe because I often thought people who had strokes would be paralyzed on at least one side of their body and their face twisted.

Then he let me in on another bomb shell. He informed me that I also had congestive heart failure. He said that my heart was only operating at 25%. I also had tachycardia (rapid heartbeat) and they thought I may have thrown a clot. They also believed that the chemotherapy I received for my breast cancer treatment, which was a cocktail of drugs, caused the heart failure.

My speech had returned to normal and I saw several doctors which included a neurologist and a cardiologist, all of whom I spoke to at length about my health history. I notified my family, church members and co-workers. The very next day, I could not speak at all! I was reduced to grunts and groans. I tried writing to communicate, but due to the stroke I lost the ability to spell. I had to really think hard to formulate words. Friends and family started calling me to check on me and were surprised because I was talking just fine the day before.

It was really hard trying to let them know that my speech had left me. It brought to my mind the story of Zacharias being struck dumb because of his unbelief. I know it wasn't because of any unbelief that I had. I felt that it happened because of my UNWILLINGNESS to speak about my breast cancer survival in a large group setting. And I guess in the back of my mind speaking about it is still very hard for me and very emotional because it was such a hard time for me.

When I tell people about my experience, I often state that I welcomed death, not that I wanted to die, but for all of the sickness and pain I was going through, I would have been at peace with it if it had happened.

I never understood how people who were struggling with pain and depression and despair could just give up. I finally understood it when I went through my cancer. It is very easy to want to give up the fight and just enter into eternal rest. I had no fight left in me. I let go and let God have His will of healing and restoring me or not and I was glad when He chose to let me live on and continued to use me in His service!

I was in the hospital almost two weeks after the stroke and was seeing a speech therapist and was slowly able to speak again. Needless to say, the women's ministry had to go to plan B for breast cancer awareness month. I continued with out-patient speech therapy for about a month or so and was off work for 5 months.

I again took a hiatus from church until I was able to formulate sentences. When I finally did return, Pastor Jones acknowledged my presence and had me to come up before the congregation. He asked me if I wanted to say something and I gladly grabbed the microphone.

I thanked God for allowing me the opportunity. I thanked the congregation for their prayers, visits and phone calls and asked that they continue to pray for me as I was diagnosed with congestive heart failure. I then stated that I am still here, and it's by the grace of God! Pastor Jones prayed for me and my continued recovery.

"I am a living testimony. I thank the Lord I'm still alive!" (The Williams Brothers) I have the experience of surviving breast cancer burned into my memory. Not because I want to remember what I went through, but because I want to remember what God delivered me from. How God was my strength when I was weak. How He was my food when I was hungry. He was my mind regulator when I thought I was losing my mind and had thoughts of giving up. He was my peace in a time of storm and my rest when I was restless. "Come unto me all ye who are burdened and heavy laden, and I will give you rest." Matthew 11:28. I will end my story with my favorite gospel song by Vashawn Mitchell. "I've Been Through Too Much Not To Worship Him!"

About Patricia E. Manning

Patricia E. Manning has resided all of her life in Houston, Texas. She has been an active member in service at New Mount Calvary Missionary Baptist Church since 1987. She has two sons and enjoys spending time with her nieces and nephews. She has a God-given love and compassion for animals.

Patricia earned a Bachelor's of Science degree in Criminal Justice and has worked for the past 18 years for the State of Texas, first as a caseworker and then as a supervisor for the past 11 years. She has a passion for both reading and writing. This is her first published work. She is also a living and breathing example of God's grace and mercy as she is a Type 1 diabetic since the age of 24, a breast cancer survivor of 5 years and a stroke survivor with a diagnosis of congestive heart failure. Patricia believes that every day she wakes up, it is because of His grace and mercies that are new every morning!

THEREFORE; *Forgive. Love. and. Rest*

DELORES MCLAUGHLIN

"For by grace are ye saved through faith;

and that not of yourselves:

It is the gift of God."

Ephesians 2:8

Releasing the Pain of the Past

Knocking on the door of my stepfather's home I felt a bit of uneasiness. My skin felt hot and my heart was racing with the vibration of quick thuds in my chest. The verbal abuse that he had subjected me to over the years was closer than I wanted it to be right now. I realized that my stepfather had good reason for wanting to talk with me about how badly he treated me growing up and wanting me to forgive him. I was surprised that he had called and asked me to come over. Especially since we had not talked to each other in over 15 years. But I questioned the motive behind the "now talk" gathering. My mind wandered back to our history while I was growing up and how I wish our relationship could have been better. However, I thought of many reasons why our relationship was defective, but it wouldn't change what had already happened between us.

The verbal abuse was extensive with my stepfather yelling at me and my brothers, "Get out of the living room and finish your chores!"

My brothers and I would chime in together, "We've already finished our chores."

176

Then my stepfather yelled, "Go in your room anyway, and I will tell you when you can come out."

My stepfather would offer my two younger sisters ice cream or anything that he chose to eat out of the refrigerator, but when my brothers and I would ask, "Can I have some ice cream?"

My stepfather would immediately reply, "No, you can't have any ice cream."

I'd ask my stepfather, "Why can't I have some ice cream?"

My stepfather growled, "Because I said so, that's why."

I would begin to cry feeling left out watching my sisters enjoy the ice cream that I wanted to taste so badly. But my three brothers would not say a word, they just sat there in silence while my stepfather continued saying negative remarks about my brothers' and my darker complexion compared to his and asked us, "Why are you all so dark? Did you get left in the sun too long?"

My mother worked long hours going in at 6 a.m. and getting home about 6 p.m. My mother would ask me and my brothers, "How was your day?"

My brothers and I would respond, "It was okay." My brothers and I had decided that we did not want our mother to worry and we decided not to say anything about our experiences with our stepfather.

Until one day, on a Friday afternoon my stepfather got angry at me because I forgot and left the refrigerator door slightly open and he said, "Why did you leave the refrigerator open?"

I said to him, "I thought I had shut it; I did not mean to, it was an accident."

As my stepfather got closer to me I began to cry and said to him, "I am sorry."

He replied, "I am tired of you not doing what I tell you to do."

The last thing I remembered was that my stepfather pushed me into the hall closet door so hard that I was inside of the closet and there was a hole left in the door. My three brothers came to my rescue and began to hit my stepfather on his legs and stomach. By the grace of God my mother came home early and witnessed what had just happened.

My mother screamed, "John what are you doing? How can you treat the children like this?"

My stepfather said, "I am tired of being disrespected by these bad kids, I am leaving."

My mother replied, "You are a grown man and you can leave, but I will not have you mistreat the children."

My stepfather left, admitting that he was in love with another woman. He divorced my mother two months later and our home environment changed to a peaceful one.

Years later, I found myself at his doorstep. I stood at the door waiting for a response from my long awaited knock when finally my stepfather opened the door with a wide grin and said, "Come in, I am glad to see you. How are you doing?"

I responded with a slow and curious look, "I am doing fine. How are you?"

He motioned me to sit on the blue couch that was next to the window. I could feel the warmth of the sun as it peeped through the window shades. I tried to look as relaxed as possible by shifting my sitting position and leaning on the arm of the couch, but I was far from being at ease. As we continued to engage in conversation, I looked at the clock and how slowly the hands seemed to be moving. I thought to myself, is this really how I want to spend my Sunday afternoon? Why should I listen to him anyway? After all, he wasn't the nicest or most understanding person when I was growing up.

My stepfather sat down on the couch next to me and began to reminisce about my growing up and said, "I remember when you were a little girl and how shy you were. You would go stand in the corner sucking your two fingers and not saying a word to anyone."

My stepfather continued talking but my mind had regressed back into the past of being that 12-year-old isolated girl. I was no longer listening to him. Why did he have to bring this up? Even though I was 26-years-old at the time, the pain was still real in my heart.

That's when my stepfather told me about his illness. He asked for forgiveness. And since I wanted to be able to move on with my life, I was willing to release the past.

The tears began to roll down my cheeks. My stepfather looked at me and said,
"Please don't cry. I am sorry that I have caused you so much pain." I wish things could have been different with me being a man and taking care of my family."

But it wasn't over yet. I felt useless as I tried to fight off the pain. Once again, the pain of feeling unloved, rejected and powerless had found me. How dare he talk about my desire to be isolated? I had no choice but to withdraw because of his ongoing verbal abuse. I realized at that moment that I was emotionally stricken with the problem of living in the past. I was tortured, broken and stuck in a dark and unforgiving place in my life. However, I realized I needed help to find peace in my life and forgive the past.

I was a victim of my past. I was detached from the reality of my subdued pain toward my stepfather, which left me in a state of emotional darkness. Even though, I was married to a good man with two children who loved me unconditionally, I was still missing something in my life. I was a stay at home mom for about a year, went to church occasionally and thought my life was moving along fine. But something was wrong.

What was I missing in my life? Why hadn't I figured it out? I was missing the truth in my life of denying what had happened to me growing up with my stepfather and I was refusing to expose the darkness that I was dealing with daily. I felt ashamed, broken-hearted and a need to prove something to others especially male figures.

The dark place was denying what had happen to me and looking in the mirror every day wanting some peace in my life. My director told me one day at work that I seemed upset and then he said, "I noticed your face looked like it had a scar on it, but then I realized that it was just your expression." I said to my director, "What do you mean by that?" My director mumbled, "I did not mean anything bad, I am sorry if that offended you." I began to feel familiar hurt of having my stepfather talk to me in a negative way.

The problem was I thought I could figure out my life instead of allowing Jesus Christ to be my guide. I read my bible regularly and prayed, but what I felt inside of me came out emotionally in my thinking, feelings and behavior. After many years of trying to forget the pain of my past, I attempted to live a normal life which was actually abnormal.

I was raised in a Christian home with my mother being a faith preacher. We traveled nationally with my mother preaching the word of God. My mother taught and raised me and my brothers in a love-based environment knowing and living the love of Jesus Christ.

My mother remarried my stepfather when I was 11 years old. My stepfather seemed to really care about me and my brothers, but not for long. A year later my mother was pregnant and my stepfather's attitude and behavior changed, especially after the birth of my sister. Even though my stepfather said he was an evangelist, his behavior proved otherwise.

The verbal abuse in the family never pulled me away from the fact that I was a Christian, but it drew me closer to Jesus Christ, letting me know that I was protected by the Lord, me and my brothers. Although I was a young girl, my mother had taught me and my brothers about the love of Jesus Christ when we were able to understand.

The Bible teaches that we will have pain, and by the grace of God He will carry us through.

After turning 18, I began to drift away from what I knew was the right thing to do and started exploring other alternatives to establish my freedom. I was lost. My life was my life and I stopped spending time with God, but chose to go out with friends, meet new potential boyfriends and go to night clubs and have several drinks to explore my freedom.

In other words, I had left behind being an example of Jesus Christ and decided to do things my way, a reflection of being stuck in the past.

After graduation from nursing school I was invited to attend a nursing graduation party that was hosted by one of the female graduates. The party was in Houston, Texas in an area of town that I was unfamiliar with, but I decided to go anyway. My husband was out of town and had given me the okay to go meet with my peers for the graduation party.

The party was in a small area of the house that was overflowing with graduate nurses and other individuals who had been invited. I mingled and met many new people, including men and women trying to have a good time. However, I was tired and decided I was going home early.

My car was parked in the front of the house but to my surprise the car would not start. I attempted to start the car again when a man walked up to my car and said, "Hi, my name is Paul. Do you need help starting your car?"

I said, "Sure."

Paul said, "What seems to be the problem?"

I said, "The car was fine when I came to the party but maybe it is the battery."

Paul raised the hood of the car and within a few minutes he said, "Try starting the car."

My car started and I thanked Paul for getting it going for me.

Paul then said, "Can you give me a ride to my car right down the street?"

I did not hesitate and said, "Sure, no problem."

Paul sat in the front with me and I drove and followed his instructions but the further I drove, the fewer houses I saw. I finally said to Paul as we were approaching the railroad tracks. "Where is your car? I don't see any cars?"

Suddenly, Paul grabbed my hair pulling my head back against the car seat and said "Drive or I will slit your throat."

I began to scream.

Paul said, "Shut up before I shut you up."

I begged Paul, "Please don't hurt me; I will do whatever you want me to do."

Paul said, "Pull over there and stop the car."

I began praying silently to God to spare my life and let me see my two-year-old daughter again.

There was a calmness that came over me and I heard God say, "Don't scream, cooperate and I will protect you."

There was a dullness that came over my entire body.

I faintly heard Paul say, "Lay down on the back seat," as he attempted to pull my clothes off.

There was no struggle and no screams from me because I remembered what God had told me to do and I knew that I could trust him.

Paul glared at me and noticed I was not reacting and I laid there quiet and still. He ordered, "Get up, get behind the wheel and drive. I don't want to hurt you."

I said to Paul, "Please let me go home to be with my baby."

I continued to drive and then Paul said, "Drive where your baby is." As I approached the long dirt drive-way to the babysitter's house.

Paul said to me, "Get out! Get out now!"

I got out of the car and felt that he was going to come grab me and pull me back into the car, but that did not happen. I walked quickly to the front door of my babysitter's house, knocked on the door and did not look back at my car or Paul. My babysitter, Vicki came to the door; I immediately ran inside, locked the door, started crying and called the police.

Paul drove my car away and three days later my car was found abandoned, leather seats were cut up and every window in the car was broken. I always think that could have been me in that car cut up and left to be found, but by the grace of God, my life was spared. Amen!

This incident happened to me 41 years ago and every day I wake up thanking Jesus Christ for sparing my life. I have been blessed to raise my daughter and son, enjoy my six grandchildren and the rest of my family and friends. This is an experience I could never take credit for—what I did or didn't do—because I know that it was by the grace of God that he led me to safety. After this happened to me, I confessed my sins to Jesus Christ and repented for all my sins. I realize that past experiences are necessary to get closer to Christ, knowing that he will use them to teach you about forgiveness, love, and emotional healing and deliverance.

Most of you reading this story would probably say what you would have done in this situation, but I know without a doubt following God's plan was my only way of survival and emotional healing. If we listen and follow God's plan, he will guide us throughout our entire lives, but we must listen to him.

This story is about releasing the path of past hurts and pain through forgiveness in becoming a vessel God can use. John 3:16 lets us know "God so loved the world that he gave his only begotten son that whosoever believeth in him should not perish but have everlasting life." Jesus Christ died for our sins and did not look back at the ill treatment that he received from those who persecuted him, but instead Jesus Christ continued to love and forgive.

I witnessed many Christians asking the question, "Why can't I have a fulfilled life?" and "What have I done to be in this awful position?" What so many Christians totally ignore is the reality of feeling lost, broken and guilty of a situation that they have no control over. Faith is standing on the word of God and not getting stuck in the past.

When we are unable to let go of the past there can be an emotional and spiritual death. What has happened behind us in the past motivates what is ahead of us. Therefore, the past is relevant to where we are trying to go in the Lord.

There are six steps to a life of releasing the pain of the past: Saved By the Grace of **God**:

1. Confess your sins to Jesus Christ regarding your past, knowing that Jesus Christ can deliver you by walking in the light of his word and living in freedom. (Romans 10:9)

2. Repent of your past sins, knowing that Jesus Christ who is your healer. There is no emotional healing without a true relationship with Jesus Christ.

3. Read God's word daily. The word of God will allow you to know him and change the way you see and think about the world. In other words, the word of God will renew how you think about life and how to approach life from God's perspective. (Psalm 16:11).

4. Grieve your losses of the past to move forward to the present time. You must be open to release whatever is holding you back to regain the new.

5. Live a present-driven life instead of a past-driven life: Live in the now instead of the past.

6. Obey God and follow his directions no matter what the circumstances are and God will do the rest.

As a result of meeting with my stepfather he apologized for treating me and my brothers the way he did both the verbal and physical abuse. I also shared with my stepfather how I felt about how he treated me growing up. My stepfather said, "I appreciate you coming over to see me and I am really sorry about all the pain I caused you. I love you and want a relationship to try to be the father I never was."

My stepfather confessed and repented and renewed his relationship with Jesus Christ that same day of our meeting. I was thankful for every moment of our time together before he went home to be with the Lord in 2006.

Lastly, Paul was never found or prosecuted. My car was a total loss but who cares about the materialistic things of life when you have God with eternal offerings that are guaranteed. I was saved by the grace of God and I am still thanking God for physical safety and emotional healing.

Remember: Christ wants us to release the hurt and pain of the past and regain freedom in him and "We can only be saved by the grace of God."

About Delores McLaughlin

Delores Ramsey McLaughlin is a motivational speaker who can inspire audiences from corporate to faith-based. She has the gift of making the most serious topics become less intimidating and more accepting. Delores is the founder and executive director of "All Out Communication" and the Pastor of "Freedom-N-Christ Global Ministries." She teaches effective communication skills, conflict resolution, collaboration and leadership skills, and strategies to successfully pursue your dreams and how to bridge gaps between cultural and religious differences.

Delores' passion lies in communicating on all levels to maintain effective, productive business and personal relationships. She has a Bachelor's degree in Communications; Master's in Business Leadership and is pursuing her Doctorate in Organizational Leadership and Development.

Delores is currently an educator teaching interpersonal and public speaking, a cardiac nurse, and the radio host of "Leading Steps in Living a Godly Life Broadcast."

She also enjoys writing and has authored "Freely Living a Godly Life," co-authored "Pursuing your Passion," "It's Never Too Late," "Remembering Dolores" and is a writer for Life Choices Magazine. She also enjoys professional membership with the National Speakers Association. Delores believes that all things are possible in Christ remembering that every good gift and every perfect gift is from above. (James 1:17).

ROD PRICE

Our sense of joy, satisfaction, and fulfillment in life
increases, no matter what the circumstances, if we are in the
center of God's will.
~Billy Graham

A Man Still Significant In My Singleness

Are you a satisfied single person?

How you view your single status will impact the way you live your life. If you view your singleness from a state of aloneness, then you are not capitalizing on the opportunities you have to be a satisfied single person. I will utilize my own life and biblical truths as a basis for this conversation. My prayer is that you will view your singleness as an opportunity to be a victorious Christian for God's Kingdom. I can tell you that I haven't always made the right choices and decisions, but addressing those growth opportunities has made me a better person today. You are not God's second choice. You are God's best!

Many words, thoughts, and ideas come to mind when you think about the word, "single." The carnal mind tends to dwell on words such as loneliness, depressed, sell-out, confused, selfish, or independent. However, these words don't give a true picture of the life of a single person who recognizes that their life has significance. From most of the world's perspective, singleness is viewed as an opportunity to do everything you want to do and not have to give an account to anyone because you are single. You can make your own choices and the mistakes made because of those choices, usually only impact you. That's an easy way of looking at the subject of singleness.

However, the true definition of "single", for the basis of our conversation means "to not be married". It's very simple. If you are not married, you are single. Some people would beg to differ. They believe that once you have placed a ring on the finger; you're no longer single. The ring represents your commitment to the other person; however, you are still single in God's eyes. Until you say, "I do," you are still considered to be single. This means you cannot behave in a married way if you are not married. You must still function as a single person with a purpose in your singleness.

I chose to be single for most of my life because I never felt adequate. In my first book, *Weight, Wait a Minute,* I give specific details regarding my singleness as it relates to me being overweight. I felt as though no one wanted me so I never expressed any feelings toward women until I was more comfortable with my size. In 1996 I lost over 100 pounds. I felt better about myself after losing the weight and this is when my relationship and dating focus began to take shape.

So, you might be wondering, "Rod, why are you still single"? My story is fairly simple, but complex in substance. I have been single for all 42 years of my life. I have never been married, engaged, nor do I have any children. I have been involved in two serious relationships in my life that could have led to marriage, but I chose to walk away from those relationships. In hindsight, I probably made a premature mistake with the first relationship, and made the right choice with the second relationship. In my first relationship that could have led to marriage; I was around 24 or 25 years old, but I thought I was ready to be married. The woman I was dating wanted to finish school before settling down.

However, I wanted to be married because I reasoned that it was the right thing to do. I had a relationship with God, but I was also young and wanted to fulfill the lusts of my flesh. We were intimate, and I also knew it was wrong. Nevertheless, once the flesh took over there appeared to be no turning back. I felt the best alternative was to get married so that the "marriage bed" would no longer be defiled. I believe had I stayed in the relationship, we would have continued to be intimate and it would have caused greater problems down the road. Another reason I chose to walk away was because I felt she was too quiet and never really gave an opinion on certain matters. Whenever I would ask a question; the response was usually, "Whatever you want is fine with me." This is one of those reasons why it's best to obey the Spirit rather than the flesh. Now, did I make the right choice? I'm not sure about that. It could have been a turning point to put me on the right path.

From that point on; I have become celibate. I can truly say God has kept me. So from a spiritual renewal perspective; I guess it was the right decision. However, "it does take two to tango." I was wrong! As the man, I take the lead and the woman follows. So I led her down that path. When I decided to walk away, it was hard because she had given up something for my sake. When a woman has been good to you and has given of herself to you in some way, especially sexually, walking away is one of the most hurtful things you could ever do. She was hurt and so was I. But the type of pain a woman feels after being jilted by a man; one can only imagine. I learned a tough lesson and failed in many relationships thereafter. She could have been the one for me and I could be living an awesome life with a great family. Ah, but God said otherwise! He has done some amazing things in me and through me as a single man.

The second relationship was quite different. We were both "into" each other, but there was no physical intimacy. I was around 31 by then. I had learned a lot from past relationships and vowed to never make the same mistake again as it relates to sex. She and I were both on the same page in that matter. We both had made commitments to God to wait until we were married to have sex with our mate. The problems commenced when we began to learn more about each other. Based on various red flags, advice from my pastor and having received revelation from God, I decided to step away from the relationship. We had begun to talk about marriage and how we would merge our lives moving forward. I had even talked to my eldest brother about being the best man at the wedding. Again, God said otherwise! So in this particular case; I know it was the right decision. She has married and is living a fruitful life. I am still single; but my life also has significance!

Now if you were to ask me back then if I felt as though my life had significance; I would say, "It depends." Music has always been a passion of mine. I have been involved with music since I was a teenager. Music has been my "mate" even during the relationships that didn't work out. I knew I had a strong foundation in music and that nothing was going to hinder that flow in any way. I knew my life was significant to others because they were blessed by the gift of music. So I felt significant because of my music, which can be enjoyed singularly or with others. But relationships are different. A relationship takes place with another person. It is give-and-take. Relationships can be hard; especially when you have two people who like things their own way and lead independent lives. The coupling of the two lives takes time, but it is possible to have a successful relationship through the nurturing and patience of both people.

In addition, to healthy relationships, it is extremely important to know what your unique purpose is so that you can be significant regardless of whether you are single or married.

Don't ever forget this: If you don't know what your calling is, know who the God of the call is. When you have a strong relationship with God, He will tell you or show you what He has for you to do. God uses people to accomplish His work. All of us have unique giftings and abilities that God must use to build up His Kingdom. The best opportunity you have to be significant for God is to go to work for Him in your singleness.

God slammed one on me in 1992. He called me to the Bible teaching/preaching ministry. I tried hard and fast to dodge this bullet, but couldn't escape. That's another thing about God! You can run, but you can't hide! He will find you right where you are! So I stopped running and accepted the call. This catapulted me into a new area that I really wasn't feeling at the time. But God said otherwise! Don't be afraid of your calling. Don't let the title of the call frighten you. For example, being a minister does not mean that you are to become a pastor. It means that God wants you to be his mouthpiece in some capacity. It's one thing to accept the call. The next step is to find out in what capacity God wishes to use you.

I am not a pulpit preacher. I get frightened to no end when I have to preach in the pulpit. But if you catch me in the classroom; I'm in my comfort zone. I can rock and roll in a classroom, because I know that my true passion is teaching. I also excel in counseling. I am a certified Christian Counselor as well. So ponder this for just a moment, and think of it as a growing tree. When a tree grows, it normally grows straight up and then it branches out. So when you accept what God is calling you to, you will branch out into other areas where you can be free to grow and blossom. Don't be blindsided by titles or professions. Pray and ask God for direction. Remember, the relationship between you and God can never be thwarted. It lasts forever! He said He will never leave us nor forsake us (Deuteronomy 31:6). I turned away from my first real relationship; but God won't! Take courage and pursue a love relationship with God first and He'll direct you further! You will always be significant in your singleness when He is in control!

Let's go deeper as it relates to the subject of "Singleness" from the Apostle Paul's perspective. First Corinthians 7 verse 8 says, "Now to the unmarried and the widows I say:

It is good for them to stay unmarried, as I do. But if they cannot control themselves, they should marry, for it is better to marry than to burn with passion." This is a somewhat meaty verse, but I will try to dissect it with the help of the Holy Spirit. Again, we see in these verses that singleness simply means to be unmarried. Paul is often spoken of in the Bible as one having great wisdom and awesome character. He is credited for writing 14 letters or epistles in the New Testament. Interestingly, Paul was single also.

The Bible never speaks of Paul being married at any time. Rather than pursuing relationships and marriage, Paul devoted his time and talents to the work of Christ. He was married to his ministry. One of the most twisted sagas of all time would be the turning point of Paul's life where he went from **persecuting the church** to ministering the Word of God **to the church**. The very thing he spoke against became the pillar of his soul. He became so devoted to ministry that he was persecuted for being a lover of the Lord. He was jailed as a result, but this didn't put out the fire he had within to get the word out about this man named, Jesus!

The message here is that as a single person, Paul had more time to devote to ministry and serve others. If you want to know how you can really make a difference as a single person, serve! Find a place where you can serve and minister to others. You might say that you were not called to minister or serve. The truth of the matter is that we were *all* called to minister and serve in some way. You have to find out what works best for you. In most cases your passion will drive your purpose. Whatever you're passionate about usually thrusts you on to the purpose and plan God has for you. I didn't know what my true gifting was until I became a member of a church that focused on ministry gifts and talents.

My former church in Houston, Texas provided a course on spiritual gifts because they recognized that everyone in the church is gifted to do something for God. My spiritual gifts are Encouragement, Teaching, Leadership, Administration, and Faith. And if you think for one minute that what I'm doing now isn't tied to one or all of these gifts, then you're wrong! All of these gifts are normally active all the time. They show up in my interactions with others. They show up when I minister through song. They show up when I'm leading a department, group or ministry. And they show up when I give of my tithes and talents to

God. Paul was not busy chasing *skirts*. He was chasing *God*. That's the key. If you're chasing the opposite sex, you're not focused on what God has for you. If you're chasing after God, He will show you His purpose and total plan for your life.

I lived a scattered life when I was younger because I was chasing the wrong things. It kept me on the move, but not for God. I was moving in my own direction or where I felt was the right way to go. God changed all of this when I got to know Him. So I pray that you would get to know God and then you will know your gifting. Find out what your spiritual gifts are, link those gifts up with your passion and you will find your true purpose in life. And guess what? You can do this without a mate or a spouse. It is best to know who you are first so you can learn to love and appreciate the person God will connect you with as your mate for life! If you don't know yourself, how do you expect someone else to get to know you?

First Corinthians 7:9 is tough to grasp because it appears to be a blatant push towards marriage. It took me a while to even grasp what he was saying. But you have to put the scripture in context. Verse 8 talks about staying single as

Paul is. But we just unpacked Paul's mission and why he was single. Verse 9 basically states that if you are unable to control the lusts of your flesh/passions, then you should get married. In other words, to do what married people do requires you to be married. Single people should not allow the lusts of their flesh to lead them into sinful situations. They tame the lusts by what? Following after the heart of God as Paul did. So he tamed his lusts by doing the work of Christ.

Paul was a man just as I am. We have lusts and passions because we were created this way. I have to keep my mind on Godly things in order to be kept away from lustful things. What kept Paul from stumbling was his ministry work. Notice he didn't say that *if* you had lusts. He said *if you are unable to control the lust*; you should marry. He uses "yourself" as a metaphor for "lust". In other words, your body wants to do what your lust/passion wants to do. To control your body means you control the lusts of the flesh by the Holy Spirit. The lusts are there, they are real, and they will get the best of you if you don't make your lusts subject to the Word and rule of God.

If you are unable to control your body, you must get married because it is better for you that you marry than light the fire of lust inside of you. This is what he means by, "Burn with passion." So the choice is yours, but it can be very tricky. Is it best to seek God and do His will.

I've learned that obedience to Him helps me control my lusts and passions. His wisdom also guides us in choosing a mate. We must also ask ourselves the question: Do I get married just because I can't control my lusts?

Well, several years ago, I made the choice to tame my lusts and passions and wait for God's best. Is it difficult? Absolutely! Have I messed up before? Absolutely! But I didn't mess up to the point to where I couldn't turn around quickly and get back on track. Life as a single man is not easy. As a matter of fact, just because you get married and can have sex doesn't mean you won't face the temptation to lust after other women. Any believer who lets the flesh run unchecked will have problems, period! The *flesh has no status!*

I have seen so many brothers (men) give up on trying to live for God so they keep one leg on God's side and the other leg next to the heat! Sooner or later if you stay too close to the heat, you will eventually get burned. I suggest brothers, that we try to live a life so that God would be pleased and get the glory.

Someone is always watching us as men; especially the young boys and younger men. We must light the fire of Christ in our hearts and tame the light of passion in our lusts! It is hard, but through faith we can hold on until God says, yes!

Lastly, I want to share four main topics with you from the scriptures that I have found to be helpful in my pursuit of what God desires for me to do and become: Contentment, Loneliness, Fruitfulness, and God's divine purpose for your life.

Contentment: 1 Timothy 6:6, *But godliness with contentment is great gain.*

To be content means you are fully satisfied with your present state in life. You have no worries, no concerns, you feel accomplished, and you feel that you are at the pentacle of life. You've reached the mountain top. To get to this point in life is a major task for some. For me personally; I think I am content with where I am right now, but not satisfied with where I am right now because I know that God is taking me higher. I believe this is why Paul coupled godliness with contentment. It takes living a life so that God is pleased to have contentment. Godliness means to behave in the way God would behave.

You've probably seen the WWJD—*What would Jesus do?*—bracelets. That's what it means to live godly. You simply do what God requires and do what He would do as it relates to your walk with Him. This godliness will help you reach the place where you are truly content. This place in God gives you gains. I know there is a phenomenon today about men getting "gains" when working out. We gain muscle or we lean up. This means we are making strides to get where we want to be. I'm getting those types of gains as well. But this type of gain; He calls great gain, and it will take you far in life. These are the types of gains I want. He even puts an exclamation mark on it and says, "Great gain!" This means that the sky is the limit. You can have whatever God says you can have. This gain will help you reach your true potential in life.

Loneliness: Colossians 2:10, *And in Christ you have been brought to fullness. He is the head over every power and authority.*

First of all, please know that in Christ you are fulfilled. You won't find fulfillment in any other thing but Christ. Family will let you down, friends will walk away, jobs will fire you, boyfriends and girlfriends will get on your nerves, and sex is good until it has ended. But in Christ, you are fulfilled! Many people try to fill the emptiness of their lives with other stuff, but the only issue is that it is a temporary fix. It only lasts for a while. Anything that has an expiration date or anyone that can cease to be who you thought they were; is temporal. But God never changes. He who is the fullness of time can bring you to fullness in Him.

I try to fill my loneliness with more of God. Notice I didn't say I'm alone. I might be lonely at times, but I am never alone. I always have the Holy Spirit as a comforter. This scripture tells me that I am fulfilled and complete in Christ. I am in Christ and He is in me. Part B of the scripture tells me that Christ is the head and complete authority over everything. Since I am in Christ; I have power! I have authority over the enemy. So when I feel alone, I can rest in the assurance of knowing that Christ is there and He's bringing the heat along with Himself. So I can turn the loneliness into fulfillment because I know He has my back!

Fruitfulness: Psalm 1:3, *That person is like a tree planted by streams of water, which yields its fruit in season and whose leaf does not wither. Whatever he does prospers.*

Have you ever wondered why trees grow to be so large when they are planted by rivers? It's because the trees are receiving steady and continuous nourishment from the streams. Because of this, the trees bear fruit when they should, the leaves never break off and they continue to grow large and strong. God wants us to be the same way. We should have such a sure foundation in Christ that we avoid making bad decisions. We pray about our decisions to see what God would say. We make sure that we bear good fruit for God. We flourish in all our endeavors. We prosper in every way imaginable. To be this fruitful requires that we gain a great understanding of God's word and stay in close proximity to Him at all times. Our life might change; but like the leaves on the trees, we'll never break away from our foundation in Christ Jesus!

Finally, God has a plan for you and me! When God made man; He made us unique and in His image. He craftily created me to be like Him. God's purpose was to restore man back to Himself and through His son Jesus Christ, give eternal life to His creation. He made us for the same purpose. We were created to be a light so that others who don't know Christ can see the light of Christ in us and walk towards that light into divine newness.

Purpose for your life: Psalm 138:8, *The Lord will vindicate me. Your love, Lord, endures forever. Do not abandon the works of your hands.*

The Lord has you fully covered. Unlike insurance where there are co-pays and deductibles to meet; God gives us *full coverage* without cost to us because He paid it all. We never have to worry about an area of our lives being overlooked because God has turned a deaf ear to the issue, concern, or prayer. No! He says I have it all covered. He is fighting for me. I don't have to worry about what people do or think. He will handle it. He loves us with an everlasting love. His love is unfailing, uninhibited, unchanged and unchained. He doesn't turn His love off when we "Turn Up" sin. He keeps expressing His love for us in spite of our own selfish and lustful ways. What He purposed for you to do, He will see you through! Just know that God has you and if you have Him He'll always give you His very best!

You are still significant in your singleness! Don't you ever forget it!

About Rod Price

Minister Roderick Lamond Price was born and raised in Tyler, Texas. He began playing the organ and keyboard at age 15 and quickly learned the art of teaching multiple part harmony to choirs shortly thereafter. In 1992, he was presented with an opportunity to move to Houston, Texas to become a Minister of Music at age 19. While in Houston; he began a secular career with Chase Bank in 1996. He resided in Houston for 8 ½ years until his secular career moved him to Arlington, Texas in March of 2001.

In addition, he received the call to ministry in November of 1999, and was licensed as a Minister in August, 2000 at First Metropolitan Church in Houston. He also received a certification as a Belief Therapist through the Therapon North Institute.

Although Min. Price is known for being passionate about leadership and development; his first love will always be music coupled with ministry. He understands that his ministry of music can only be blessed and anointed when God is the focus. He enjoys teaching and developing others to reach their true potential. His first published book "Weight, Wait a Minute" was released on July 3, 2015.

He can be reached at Rod WWAM Price on Facebook or by email at rodprice.hifavored@att.net.

Were you inspired? Your hope renewed? Did you notice how God does work all things together for good? We hope you received how God takes brokenness and turns it into something beautiful when we yield our brokenness to Him.

Many of the authors in this anthology struggled with sharing and releasing their story to the world. But as we pressed through our fears and insecurities and continued to write, continued to pressed through the edits and corrections, something wonderful happened. We were set free in so many ways.

We pray that as you continue in your journey, when brokenness comes to visit you—and it will—that you place it in the hands of God. Therefore; Forgive, Love, and Rest.

And they overcame him by the blood of the Lamb,
and by the word of their testimony;
and they loved not their lives unto the death.
Revelation 12:11